Better Mental Health in Schools

Better Mental Health in Schools recognises the value of school staff in supporting mental health in children and young people and introduces new skills for enhancing the therapeutic benefits of environments and relationships in schools.

This book discusses and links to provision in schools and to supporting good mental health in pupils across four key areas for enhancing mental health and well-being – **cognition, compassion, containment**, and **connection.** Based on relevant and timely research, it provides an accessible insight into practical ways to change practice. Rather than prescribe one programme or suggest one curriculum design, the book shows how strengthening knowledge and understanding of some basic underpinnings of good mental health will scaffold the development of better mental health in schools and offers illustrations of how that could look in everyday practice.

Written for practitioners and based on many years of experience in classrooms across a variety of education provisions, this book reflects the lived, experiential perspective of a teacher and school therapist. Through paying attention to these four key areas of daily life in school, staff can create an environment that supports mental well-being while not depleting their own mental health.

Alison Woolf is a teacher and play therapist. Her experience includes teaching in university, secondary, primary, early years, and special school settings. As a school play therapist, she has worked in mainstream and SEMH provision, as well as working with looked after and adopted children. Alison is a director of Better Play Ltd., which offers training for school teams in counselling skills in schools, trauma, attachment, and therapeutic play. She is a registered member of the British Association of Play Therapists (BAPT) a clinical supervisor, filial therapist and author of *Better Play! Practical Strategies for Supporting Play in Schools for Children of All Ages*.

Better Mental Health in Schools

Four Key Principles for Practice in Challenging Times

Alison Woolf

LONDON AND NEW YORK

Cover image: © Getty Images

First published 2023
by Routledge
4 Park Square, Milton Park, Abingdon, Oxon OX14 4RN

and by Routledge
605 Third Avenue, New York, NY 10158

Routledge is an imprint of the Taylor & Francis Group, an informa business

© 2023 Alison Woolf

The right of Alison Woolf to be identified as author of this work has been asserted in accordance with sections 77 and 78 of the Copyright, Designs and Patents Act 1988.

All rights reserved. No part of this book may be reprinted or reproduced or utilised in any form or by any electronic, mechanical, or other means, now known or hereafter invented, including photocopying and recording, or in any information storage or retrieval system, without permission in writing from the publishers.

Trademark notice: Product or corporate names may be trademarks or registered trademarks, and are used only for identification and explanation without intent to infringe.

British Library Cataloguing-in-Publication Data
A catalogue record for this book is available from the British Library

Library of Congress Cataloging-in-Publication Data
A catalog record has been requested for this book

ISBN: 978-1-032-23428-1 (hbk)
ISBN: 978-1-032-23484-7 (pbk)
ISBN: 978-1-003-27790-3 (ebk)

DOI: 10.4324/9781003277903

Typeset in Sabon
by Deanta Global Publishing Services, Chennai, India

Contents

Introduction   **1**
Terminology   3
References   4

1 The role of schools in addressing mental health and well-being   **5**
The prevalence of mental ill health in children and young people   5
The stigma of mental health in schools   7
Schools as primary sources of mental health support   8
External support services   10
Filling the gap   10
Supporting mental health in schools   13
Responding to the pandemic   15
Preparing for the future   16
Conclusion   17
References   18

2 Cognition   **25**
What is cognition?   25
Why does cognition matter for teachers' practice?   26
Understanding the causes underlying the behaviours of pupils   28
Understanding the causes underlying the behaviours of teachers   30
Cognitive approaches to better mental health in pupils   32
    Loan your adult brain   33
    Normalising   34
    Theory of parts   34
Cognitive approaches to better mental health in school staff   36
    Theory of parts   37
    Staff supervision   37
Conclusion   39
References   40

3 Compassion   **45**
What is compassion?   45
Be kind: the kindness of compassion   48
Why does compassion matter for teachers' practice?   49

v

Contents

What does compassion look like in teachers' practice?   50
   Being with   50
   Giving full attention   50
   Staying in the here and now   50
   Creating a sense of safety   51
   Curiosity   51
   Self-awareness   51
   Staying power   52
Compassion as a route to better mental health for teachers   52
Compassion as a route to better mental health for pupils   53
Conclusion   54
References   55

4 Containment 61

Holding it together   61
   Window of tolerance   62
What is emotion?   62
Mixed emotions   64
Thinking about parts   64
What is emotion regulation?   65
Attachment relationships and emotion regulation   70
Relationships in school and emotion regulation   71
Enhancing emotion regulation in the classroom   72
   Acknowledging feelings   73
Conclusion   74
References   75

5 Connection 79

Connection is key to human health and well-being   79
Attachment: a template for connection   80
   Attachment behaviours   81
   Attachment and loss   82
Being good enough   83
Therapeutic relationships in schools   84
   Therapeutic skills   86
A sense of belonging in school   88
Developing a sense of belonging   89
   Create special traditions for your class   89
   Be a person as well as a teacher   89
   Offer enduring relationships   90
   Offer a variety of activities which encourage working in groups or
      teams   90
   Allow for and recognise the value of play   90
   Creating change for a sense of belonging   91
Conclusion   92
References   93

6 What are schools for?   **99**

What is the point of education?   99
  Safeguarding knowledge for individual and collective benefit   100
  Social progress for pupils and the nation   101
  Economic growth of the nation   102
  Personal development of each pupil   103
What are teachers for?   104
  Professional expectations of teachers   105
  Being a reflective practitioner   105
  Self-awareness in the role of teacher and worker in education   106
  The golden rule   107
School as a safe space and safe spaces in schools   108
Conclusion   109
References   110

Conclusion   **115**
References   117

Index   **119**

Introduction

Better Mental Health in Schools: Four Key Principles for Practice in Challenging Times is a book about practice, written for practitioners, and based on many years of experience in classrooms across a variety of education provisions, reflecting the lived, experiential perspective of a teacher and school therapist.

The intention behind the writing of this book was to create a space for the discussion of the role of schools in providing mental health support. There is debate in the UK over how much responsibility for the mental health of school-aged children and young people should rest with education settings. It takes a village to raise a child: within the community that supports the development of the child or young person, choices over where support services for mental health are placed need to be based on how to provide the most effective service. Clarity about responsibilities and expectations across provisions is helpful for both children and young people and for those working in the different settings. Once the most helpful and effective pathway for the support of mental health in children and young people has been designed, a clear division of responsibility means proportionate funding and resourcing can be allocated.

The content is not intended as an academic thesis on theory and contemporary research. Literature from a wide range of sources provides context and supports ideas, but learning from, and for, practice in the classroom is at the heart of the book. The model of four key principles can support good mental health in everyday interactions, sustaining well-being at times of calm and tranquillity. These times build resilience for future obstacles, unpredictability, or strain. Challenging times are part of life; whether the struggles are our own individual experiences, testing times for our community, or global challenges. Understanding and compassion, managing feelings, and being in connection to others are helpful, both at the time of the challenge and in recovery.

Education settings all aspire to create the most effective learning environment possible, and 'it is widely recognised that a child's emotional health and wellbeing influences their cognitive development and learning' (PHE & DfE, 2021 p. 3). Professional teaching roles require some level of attention to the state of pupils' mental health in order to set up conditions for learning. *Better Mental Health in Schools: Four Key Principles for Practice in Challenging Time*s provides information and skills for responding to everyday fluctuations in pupil mental health needs. Acute or chronic mental health needs that are, or could be, harmful to physical and social well-being require intervention from specialist mental health professionals, be they situated in school or out of school. In a medical analogy, it is not about whether schools would ever be the Accident and Emergency service, but rather, whether, with support, they could be a minor injuries unit. Continuing with the metaphor, schools

DOI: 10.4324/9781003277903-1

Introduction

have pupils in their classrooms who are in the 'waiting room' for an appointment or on the waiting list for treatment with specialist services, and school staff support these pupils through waiting and treatment periods.

Learning about four key principles for practice to promote better mental health in the classroom offers a choice of practical and effective approaches to support pupils that feel congruent with personal attributes and beliefs. It is a 'pick and mix' approach, in which one or more of the key ways of responding to pupils can be integrated into teachers' established 'toolbox'. The chapters in the book can be read in any order, particularly the four chapters on the key principles, as each stands alone in introducing one consideration for ways to develop everyday better mental health.

Chapter 1, 'The role of schools in addressing mental health and well-being', paints a picture of the mental health needs of children and young people and of the services and provisions to meet those needs in the early 2020s in the UK. This picture provides a background for the discussion on the role of teachers and schools in supporting the mental health of pupils.

Chapter 2, 'Cognition', introduces the reader to the first key principle for supporting better mental health in pupils. Knowing more about mental health in terms of child development is helpful for our professional development. In this chapter, theories behind the link between thoughts, feelings, and behaviours lead to illustrations of additional ways to respond to pupils that may support their mental health.

Chapter 3, 'Compassion', considers the role of compassion in supporting better mental health. Compassion is intrinsic to practice in the helping professions, although possibly not often reflected on in training for teachers. Exploring current understanding of the nature of compassion, and the impacts of giving and receiving compassion, informs the illustration of practices for enhancing pupil and teacher well-being.

Chapter 4, 'Containment', explores the theory of emotion and emotion regulation, helping us to understand why regulating the emotional climate in the classroom is important. Regulating our own and pupils' emotions prepares us all for teaching and learning tasks. Helpful skills and strategies for containment, and for developing pupils' self-regulation skills, can lead to calmer classrooms, which are the foundation for learning and feeling safe in school.

Chapter 5, 'Connection', reflects on the universal human need for relationships. Positive connections to others and a sense of belonging in school are important for good mental health. Attachment theory explains how the influence of previous relationships resonates in relationships in the classroom. Understanding attachment theory and our human need for connection can shift our feelings about classroom behaviours and inform the ways we respond. Practical activities can build connections and create a sense of belonging in schools.

Chapter 6, 'What are schools for?', returns to the debate over the place of mental health support in schools by exploring the belief and ethos underpinning the provision of education in our school settings in the UK. Understanding of the rationale for education, ideological beliefs, and personal teaching style provides context for implementing the four key principles in practice in the classroom. Cognition, compassion, containment, and connection support the evolving purpose of education, and of relationships in schools, during changing and challenging times.

For some, it feels as though schools are being asked to 'step up' in terms of mental health support when it appears that other services are being 'stepped down'. Research suggests that schools do, and increasingly will, play a vital role in identifying and addressing the mental health of pupils. The recent, unprecedented school closures due

2

to the COVID-19 pandemic have highlighted what is missed by pupils, families, and communities when school provision is lost. The experience of isolation, uncertainty, loss, community anxiety, and sudden change have all added to the burden of poor mental health across all generations, in particular that of children and young people. For some, the time away from school improved their mental health. For these pupils, the return to school has challenged their emotional well-being. Understanding this underlines the need for creating feelings of safety and belonging in schools.

Through experiences with the pandemic, we have had to be responsive, move fast, adapt, and find creative solutions to new problems. These are skills we are going to have to deploy in the face of current and predicted future challenges. The acknowledgement of intergenerational trauma and historical and geo-political injustices, along with the emerging threats of further pandemics, destabilising conflicts, economic uncertainties, the effects of climate change, and the loss of biodiversity, pose challenges for us all.

Making meaning out of experiences, feeling valued, and finding purpose are essential for good mental health in teachers and pupils. In challenging times, cognition, compassion, containment, and connection become even more important. Compassion and containment for self and for others make a space for understanding, and for taking on board, what we hear as we listen to our pupils. Caring, kindness, self-regulation, and understanding build and strengthen connection. Connections in school, and attuned teacher–pupil relationships, will be anchors for any turbulent times ahead.

The debate on the role of schools in supporting mental health is increasingly relevant and important; it still may be some time before conclusions are agreed upon regarding the scope of schools in meeting the mental health needs of their pupils. It may take a lot longer before the training, resourcing, and funding are put in place to deliver mental health support in every school across the UK. Many initiatives have been announced and then abandoned or delayed. This book does not prescribe one programme or suggest one curriculum design but, rather, suggests that strengthening knowledge and understanding of some basic underpinnings of good mental health, along with illustrations of how that could look in everyday practice, will scaffold the development of better mental health in schools. The ideas do not require additional resources but provide practical ideas and support for current practice. We may, at some point, reach a universal, well-resourced, evidence-based programme for supporting good mental health in schools. Cognition, compassion, containment, and connection will always be key to any such resolution of the current debate.

Terminology

Throughout, 'pupils' refers to children in schools.

'CYP' in the content refers to children and adolescents of school age; 'CYP' in the research references may refer to anyone under the age of 25.

'Teacher' refers to anyone in an education setting involved in teaching activities or roles.

I acknowledge the terms 'pupil', 'CYP', and 'teacher' are generic and reductive. The terms are used to support the flow of the writing but are intended to represent the children, adolescents, and young people in our classrooms, as well as the dedicated staff across any of the roles that support the learning and development of those in our schools.

Introduction

References

Open Government Licence v3.0 OGL. Full details available at: https://www.nationalarchives.gov
.uk/doc/open-government-licence/version/3/

Public Health England (PHE) and Department for Education (DfE) (2021) Promoting children
and young people's mental health and wellbeing: A whole school or college approach. Retrieved
from: https://www.gov.uk/government/publications/promoting-children-and-young-peoples
-emotional-health-and-wellbeing [Accessed 20th December 2021].

Chapter 1

The role of schools in addressing mental health and well-being

The prevalence of mental ill health in children and young people

> Most children and young people have good mental health; however, a minority, around one in ten, have mental health conditions or disorders and require assessment and intervention from primary, community and secondary healthcare services.
>
> *(Welsh Government, 2000c p. 3)*

The Welsh Government remind us that we must always bear in mind most pupils we work with will have good mental health. When one in ten children need specialist mental health support, we are recognising a level of mental ill health that pervades every classroom and school group, presumably across all our home nations.

In 'The Covid Generation: A Mental Health Pandemic in the Making', the All-Party Parliamentary Group on a Fit and Healthy Childhood (2021) reported that, in 2020, one in seven pupils was likely to have a mental health disorder, an increase from 2017 when it was one in ten. The COVID-19 pandemic may have changed our understanding of needs and provisions in and out of schools. In a 2020 planned review of the 2017 NHS Digital 'Mental Health of Children and Young People in England', the researchers found that:

> Rates of probable mental disorders have increased since 2017. In 2020, one in six (16.0%) children aged 5 to 16 years were identified as having a probable mental disorder, increasing from one in nine (10.8%) in 2017.
>
> *(NHS Digital, 2020 online)*

The use of 'probable' as a measure for mental health issues could mean numbers are disputed, but is more inclusive of what many believe are the mental health needs of children and young people (CYP), as not all needs are identified in official statistics. In 2021, parents or carers of pupils in Key Stages 1, 2, 3, and 4 sought support for their child's mental health from education services (68.3%), friends and family (37.9%), and online or telephone support services (35.2%). However, 15.6% did not reach out for support from any of these sources (NHS Digital, 2021).

DOI: 10.4324/9781003277903-2

In a 2017 review, 'The First 1000 Days', the Mental Health Foundation in Wales reported that the number of referrals to Child and Adolescent Mental Health Service (CAMHS) in Wales doubled between 2010 and 2014. During a slightly later period, a report from the North Wales Social Care and Well-being Improvement Collaborative (2017) found that the number of self-harm risk assessments had doubled between 2012 and 2016. In the financial year 2012–2013 the Welsh Government funding for CAMHS was around 7% of the overall funding for mental health support services (Mental Health Foundation, 2016). In Northern Ireland (SSUNI, 2021), a similar amount of the overall percentage of the mental health budget was spent on child and adolescent mental health services in 2017. The Northern Ireland Health and Social Care Board identified a shortfall of over 20% in the funding provided for meeting the levels of mental health needs in CYP. Young Minds reported that funding intended for mental health needs in CYP had been used for other health priorities by some clinical commissioning groups (Bailey & Knightsmith, 2017).

A report released prior to the COVID-19 pandemic from Anne Longfield, the ex-Children's Commissioner for England (2020), described the volume of need for mental health support for CYP. The figure of 15- to 19-year-olds with a diagnosed mental health condition was just over one in every ten CYP or four in a typical class of 31 or 32. Based on this, Longfield estimated that we needed a mental health service that allows for close to a million CYP to access specialist services and for more than a million CYP to access help for their mental health in community settings such as schools. When pupils were asked about the scale of poor mental health in CYP of secondary school age, their responses suggested a high level of need for support. A 2019 survey of more than 12,000 secondary school age young people in England and Wales conducted by the mental health charity Mind found that one in seven respondents reported experiencing their mental health as being poor. Respondents to the survey reported that a much lower number of CYP in need had accessed designated mental health services than NHS Digital reported in 2021. Pupils have a lack of confidence in schools to address their mental health issues or provide appropriate care for their emotional well-being (Mind, 2019, 2021). Only one in five of the pupils responding to the 2019 Mind survey had accessed support for their mental health, and half of these pupils felt the support was not helpful. A 2018 survey of more than 1,000 school staff demonstrated a gap in perceptions between staff and pupils. Almost three-quarters of the school staff surveyed felt confident that pupils who needed it were being adequately supported (Mind, 2019).

A report on a survey of teachers across Scotland in 2018 (Mental Health Foundation, n.d.) found that almost three-quarters of staff felt they lacked both the training and confidence needed to support pupils' mental health. Despite our concerns around our lack of training and skill in supporting mental health, a 2016 YMCA report suggested that pupils think school staff should be taking on the role of mental health support. An evaluation of a mental health pilot in England (DfE, 2017) which aimed to improve joint working and communication between schools and NHS Children and Young People Mental Health Services, and included educating staff on referral processes and prevalent mental health challenges for CYP, demonstrated this anxiety can be addressed. The evaluation of the pilot suggested that 'the reassurance and additional support provided … often helped to alleviate anxiety that had built up, where school staff had been operating beyond the margins of their expertise' (DfE, 2017 p. 70). In 2018, only 13% of teachers in Scotland had been given mental health first-aid training (Mental Health Foundation, n.d.) in contrast to a recommendation that, by that time, a programme should have been in place to train all staff (Gordon & Platt, 2017). Kidger et al. (2021)

found that when teachers were given a programme which included mental health first-aid training to support their own mental well-being, no substantial improvements were reported. Despite these results, Kidger et al. (2021) believed that increased knowledge and understanding of mental health issues would increase staff feelings of competency and support their own good mental health and, as a result, that of their pupils.

A 2019 survey of school staff by the National Education Union (NEU), including school leaders, teachers, and support staff, identified some limitations to supporting mental health in schools. These barriers to support for pupils' mental health included:

- loss of funding
- loss of support staff
- the value placed on academic assessment
- the time pressures on teaching staff workloads
- the lack of access to mental health services in the community.

A lack of knowledge and confidence, along with shortages of time and staff, could play a part in our inability, at times, to notice the needs in our classrooms. Soneson and Ford (2020) suggested that adults involved in the lives of CYP, such as their parents or teachers, identify less than a fifth of their mental health issues.

There are disparities not only in addressing mental health needs but also in the prevalence of poor or challenging mental health across demographics. Being an older child, female, or socioeconomically disadvantaged increases the risk for developing poor mental health (Welsh Government, 2021; Children's Commissioner for England, 2020). The Centre for Mental Health's (2021) 'Children and Young People's Mental Health: The Facts' report noted the prevalence of mental health problems in young people within the youth justice system. They were three times more likely to have mental health problems than their peers not involved with the system. In his 2016 'Review of the Youth Justice System in England and Wales', Charlie Taylor reported to the government that more than one-third of children in the youth justice system in England and Wales had a diagnosed mental health problem. Ethnicity and age influence the likelihood of experiencing mental health issues as do deprivation or being involved in safeguarding systems (Deighton et al., 2019). Being looked after or accommodated also increases the likelihood of poor mental health (Gordon & Platt, 2017). Having additional learning needs makes CYP three times more likely to experience additional mental health needs (Lavis et al., 2019).

The experience of stigma around mental ill health adds another layer of challenge for struggling pupils. Stigma is the prejudicial and discriminatory belief of a person or a group that a certain attribute or characteristic is undesirable. Stigma is used to exclude or to negatively judge others based on difference.

The stigma of mental health in schools

Stigma can have as much impact on a young person as the mental health challenge itself; it can compound their mental health struggles and mean that they are less likely to seek out help or support (Ahmedani, 2011; Corrigan & Watson, 2002; Mental Health Foundation, 2021). A survey by the YMCA (2016) highlighted that the effects of stigma on young people in education were detrimental to their relationships, attendance, and academic progress. Schools' responsibilities include ensuring attendance and academic progress, and these areas of our roles are constantly monitored by both schools and governments. The negative impact of stigma on relationships in schools is not measured and given targets in quite the same way. Many of us do not need targets to tell us that relationships in schools underpin achievement and attendance, well-being, and feelings of safety and belonging. The Welsh Government have acknowledged the importance of relationships in education settings.

> Developing positive relationships between a teacher and learner is a fundamental aspect of quality learning and teaching. The effects of teacher–learner relationships have been researched extensively, and point to how positive relationships can have good social and academic outcomes.
>
> *(Welsh Government, 2021 p. 17)*

A further detrimental outcome of stigma, particularly during adolescence when the developmental task of identity formation is key, is that the young person who experiences negative judgements from peers, or being labelled or alienated within their wider society, may absorb these views into their own sense of their developing identity (Gibson, 2022). The YMCA (2016) survey found that pupils believed teachers should play a role in supporting their mental health; however, just under a third of the CYP reported that staff were perpetrators of stigma. This finding is shocking and troubling.

In order to address the stigma experienced around mental health issues, it is important to reflect on our use of language when referring to mental health. Mental health, like physical health, is a state that we all have all the time. For most of us, this may fluctuate between good health and ill health. In a paper entitled 'The Elephant in the Room', Danby and Hamilton (2016) researched the stigma attached to the term 'mental health' in primary schools. They found that staff perceived a stigma in the use of the term 'mental health' and that other terms were preferred by staff, such as 'well-being'. Staff felt that using terms such as 'well-being' was less challenging than the term 'mental health' (Danby & Hamilton, 2016). These findings are interesting and give us food for thought. If we do not use the term 'mental health', we teachers, and our CYP, cannot become comfortable with the language. Choosing alternative language to 'mental health' suggests some level of taboo within society around the term. As a society, we need to consider and address a hesitancy about naming emotional well-being issues as issues of mental health. The less comfortable we are in talking about mental health, the less we use the words themselves, the more stigmatising the term can become.

Schools as primary sources of mental health support

The data and opinion from academic experts help to inform the discussion as to whether it is our role to meet the need for mental health support in CYP. Considerations may be about whether we can, and whether the governments across the UK and elsewhere are prepared to provide the resources for schools to take on this role. It is an important discussion yet to be resolved.

How do we feel about being asked to:

- identify pupil's mental health status
- respond to their mental health needs
- know how, when, and where to refer on?

We may be all too aware of our own anxieties about having a role in each of these areas; we fear making mistakes, stigmatising pupils or certain ways of being, and exposing our own biases, and we may feel concern about the impacts of any such role on our own mental health. We seek and need more clarity around expectations, responsibilities, and resources. 'In England, recent policy directives have mandated an increased role of schools to promote and protect child and adolescent mental health' (Mansfield et al., 2021 p. 2). Clarity around this role is not always evident, although some new additional responsibilities are clearer: the introduction of designated mental health leads in schools and the inclusion of teaching mental health in the school curriculum in England (Mansfield et al., 2021). The guidance in Wales on embedding a whole-school approach to mental health and well-being included a description of expectations of teacher's knowledge and skills.

> Being taught by highly trained, highly motivated, trauma-informed teachers who are aware of the impact they have on the young person's overall development, inside and outside the classroom, is central to promoting emotional and mental well-being.
>
> *(Welsh Government, 2021 p. 17)*

This may be less amenable to measurement than the guidance in England for numbers of mental health leads in schools and curriculum resources for teaching about mental health.

Schools need to have appropriate resources in place if we are to be tasked with supporting mental health needs in our pupils. Many of us feel that we are either already being asked, or expected, to do this, or we are doing this because it is part of how we work. The level of mental health need we can address is important to consider when supporting pupils.

> We wouldn't expect GPs [general practitioners] to do the work of consultants, but I feel that we are expecting teachers, as general practitioners, to do the work of experts.
>
> *(National Assembly for Wales, 2018 p. 48).*

Providing mental health support for all is a different role from providing specialised mental health support requiring specialist input. Teachers are not alone in feeling that they lack training and knowledge in supporting mental health needs in their pupils. Young Minds (2019) carried out a survey with GPs and practice nurses who described a lack of skills and confidence in responding to mental health needs in CYP. Many respondents felt that they sometimes work outside of their area of expertise and knowledge when supporting CYP with mental health issues, and there was also a lack of faith among some that any referral to CAMHS would necessarily lead to appropriate treatment responses (Young Minds, 2019). It may be surprising to hear that we are not alone in our feelings of uncertainty around whether we should be responding to mental health needs in pupils and whether we are capable of doing so. A 2017 Care Quality Commission report laid bare many faults with mental health services for CYP in England. They reported that, across services, including education, acute medical care settings, and community doctors' clinics, practitioners may not have the professional skills to assess needs or accurately refer on. The sense of being 'out of our depth' has often seemed exacerbated by our experiences of lack of support from external services. These providers of mental health support that we perceived as trained and competent

Mental health and the role of schools

can be seen in the context of their own struggles with getting adequate support and of their feelings of inadequacy to the task (Shelemy et al., 2019).

The British Psychological Society (BPS) (in National Assembly for Wales, 2018) reported that teachers are better placed to support mental health, as key adults in a pupil's life, than a specialist who sees a child for an hour a week. They acknowledged the excellence of school staff responses to mental health needs in students. The Care Quality Commission (CQC, 2017) agreed that the value of the mental health support provided in schools is widely recognised. The BPS did, however, report finding school staff unsure of what to do and what to say and afraid of 'getting it wrong' (National Assembly for Wales, 2018). The consensus appeared to be that teachers, while responding and making a difference, do not feel adequate to the role of mental health supporter and fear 'making things worse'. Head teachers' representatives highlighted concern about what is expected of teachers, likening it to putting their finger in the dyke to hold back an impending flood of need (National Assembly for Wales, 2018). The debate as to where support for mental health needs is provided can be characterised as a simple choice between schools and health services. A blended provision in which education and health services work together to provide a cohesive wrap-around mental health response might feel like it could provide a safe and effective resolution to current deficiencies. Such a support system would require addressing extensive and systemic shortfalls in training and resourcing as well as communication and access.

External support services

Public Health England (PHE) (2016) reported that only 25% of CYP were able to access treatment for mental health issues when needed. Ease of access to CAMHS is not a new issue for many of us. The criteria for referral to CAMHS relies on the mental health difficulty being serious and of a complex and lasting nature (CCHP, 2007). It can feel as though 'only risk of harm to self or others' meets the assessment requirements for acceptance for an intervention. In 2017, Hobby reported that cuts to local authority budgets had impacted CAMHS and that this meant that the threshold for accessing an intervention has markedly increased.

A report on a pilot for reforming mental health services for CYP found a slightly lower level of access to services than PHE (2016), with less than a quarter of those in need being able to access appropriate provisions (Rocks et al., 2020). Improving speed of access to CAMHS, as well as increasing the extent of their services, would require substantial funding. Reforming services could lead to either decreased time waiting for an initial appointment or better treatment options, but probably not both (Rocks et al., 2020). A report card for CAMHS in England might record 'Not good enough'. Young people informed a review of services by the CQC (2017) of their frustration and concern over waiting times. The report identified that over 40% of CAMHS services in England either required improvement or were inadequate.

Filling the gap

What happens when services such as CAHMS cannot address the huge need for mental health services for CYP? Hobby (2017) felt that schools fill the gap. He warned that, while schools are good at doing this, it may hide the truth that services are under-funded and under-resourced, as the need seems to be addressed. Teachers face a dilemma in addressing the mental health needs of pupils; they may want to help or feel obliged to help but do not want that help to mask the need for more and better specialist support services. Hobby (2017) suggested that giving schools and teachers messages about their value and success in supporting mental health ignores the emotional costs to teachers and resourcing costs to schools in doing so. During the COVID-19 pandemic, some schools prioritised basic needs over educational aims. Teachers and school senior management teams understand that hungry, cold, anxious pupils will not be ready to learn. If no one is meeting a pupil's basic needs for physical and psychological well-being, schools cannot do their job of educating. Schools may take on additional roles not as a matter of policy or because of explicit external direction but, rather, through an understanding of how and when children learn and the experience that no one else is meeting their pupils' needs that are a pre-requisite to learning. Schools meeting basic needs may be through necessity rather than choice.

Soneson and Ford (2020) place us at the heart of mental health support for CYP, finding schools were the place where mental health support is most frequently accessed. They suggested teachers in schools are the people most likely to identify mental health issues. It is a big responsibility for school staff to see in black and white that schools are *the* most common place where mental health needs are identified and supported. Schools may not be the most common place where physical health needs are identified and responded to. Many of us will have experiences of being the ones who alert external services to failure to thrive or physical neglect. We also have sometimes discussed with families our concerns around physical injuries or delays and differences in physical skills and development. What we have not felt was that we teachers have been at the forefront of support for physical health. The difference in expectations of schools in mental health support raises huge questions around budgets and status and understanding and expectations of what the roles of CAMHS and education services are in our society.

Where in our education system provisions are made for supporting better mental health is a question if budgets are limited or the will to provide services appears to be lacking. There is much evidence to suggest that mental health issues, or the underlying susceptibility for them, often develop early in life. Although in Wales, secondary schools have been required to provide a school counselling service since 2008 (Welsh Assembly Government, 2008), a pilot at primary schools, which showed some promising results (Pattison et al., 2011), was not followed up. This is despite the then Health Secretary in England, Jeremy Hunt, stating that the aim for mental health services for CYP was to ensure mental health problems were identified and treated as early as possible to prevent them becoming more serious (DoHSC & DfE, 2017). Both Northern Ireland (Northern Ireland Direct, n.d.) and Scotland (Scottish Government, 2020) have prioritised counselling services for secondary-age pupils; in Scotland, as in Wales, this includes Year 6 pupils in primary schools. This is despite the evidence suggesting that half of long-term mental health problems will become evident before the age of 14 (Gordon & Platt, 2017; House of Commons Education and Health Committees, 2017; Welsh Government, 2021). The reticence to spend budgets on counselling interventions in primary schools means we are missing both health benefits for pupils, wider social benefits for schools and communities, and the economic benefits of future savings on reactive spending needed later on for more entrenched mental health challenges in adolescents and young adults (Finning et al., 2021).

Early intervention for a mental health vulnerability or struggle means providing support in primary schools and nurseries, as well as in secondary schools and colleges.

Mental health and the role of schools

Training across the whole workforce and consistent provision of interventions through primary, secondary, and tertiary settings in supporting mental health, would mean:

- catching difficulties early
- following vulnerable and challenged pupils throughout the course of their education
- cohesion of approach, ethos, and care.

Across all areas of education provision, teachers encounter a range of mental health states. Referring to a study by the teachers' union NASUWT, an article in the *Independent* newspaper (Pells, 2017) reported that close to 100% of staff in the study had contact with pupils who they believe are experiencing a mental health difficulty. Just under half of the respondents in the study had ever received training on dealing with mental health issues in pupils.

We are all trained regularly in responding to safeguarding issues. One key response is to listen before passing on or referring on. If a child discloses to you, you take that responsibility and have training in listening, not leading, and in believing and acknowledging the experience of the child. The same training and understanding needs to be given for responding when a child discloses feeling anxious, sad, or angry. We know that deflecting a child who is trying to tell us something difficult, which they may not have shared before, can lead to the child not talking about it again. The 'No Wrong Door' policy in Wales (Children's Commissioner for Wales, 2020) suggested just such an approach. Whoever the child chooses to go to is the first point in any response to their needs. The Children's Commissioner for Wales wanted all services in Wales to respond to the 'No Wrong Door' policy. Wherever a child first seeks help, they will be accepted into the joined-up system rather than being sent somewhere else. This would address a concern that a lack of integration in provisions leads to CYP being 'bounced' from service to service (Welsh Government, 2020c). The outcomes of intentions for a joined-up service provision, in response to previous reports and crises in the UK, have not met our hopes and expectations.

Asking teachers to plug a gap without providing them with resources may prove to be a recipe for increasing staff mental health issues. A government green paper on mental health in England, 'Failing a Generation' (House of Commons, 2018), warned that any decision to ask more of schools in terms of meeting mental health needs, without providing additional resources, would put significant pressure on the teaching workforce. Time, money, knowledge, skills, and support for the supporters are all essential if schools are to take on roles which currently, officially, reside in health and social care services. In 2019, the Mental Health Foundation in England's 'State of a Generation' report, while acknowledging schools and school staff as important sources of support for mental health, also warned of the detrimental impact of schools and staff that do not support children appropriately.

A 2018 statement from the National Assembly for Wales (NAW) summarised what needs to be in place for pupils to receive the timely help that will make a difference and give staff the confidence and expertise to respond, which they identify is currently missing:

- training in mental health awareness for the whole of the education workforce
- awareness and understanding of stigma
- knowledge of support services and how to refer on.

Schools are at the centre of children's lives, and their emotional well-being and good mental health is often being addressed in schools, yet it is not universally acknowledged that schools need additional funding, training, and professional health service support to achieve the outcomes we all want for our CYP. In 2021, the UK Parliament stated that 'the number of mental health support teams in schools and colleges will grow from 59 to 400 by April 2023, supporting nearly 3 million children', which will be about 35% of pupils in England. From April 2023, 65% of pupils in England will still not be in schools and colleges with mental health support teams.

There have been many promises, pilots, and programmes for schools, such as Targeted Mental Health in Schools (TaMHS) (DCSF, 2008), Future in Mind (Department of Health, 2015), and Mental Health First Aid Training (Gov.UK, 2017). These have not led to significant, enduring, comprehensive changes across our education settings. When projects have been promoted or piloted, feedback has not been universally positive. Planned programmes do not always materialise, or timescales slip. The promised first-aid training for primary schools was dropped, and the Department for Health and Social Care reported that feedback from busy schools led to their decision (Booth, 2021). Feedback on mental health first-aid training for secondary schools included one opinion that the training offered nothing new and that the programme itself was a hollow and token response to the training needs of schools (NEU, 2019). Doing our best with what we have is a holding position while we wait for effective, resourced, universal programmes to be implemented.

Supporting mental health in schools

We are asked to climb mountains every day in our school settings: meet this target, achieve these outcomes, cover this content, and keep classrooms calm and on-task. We fill in paperwork before and after lessons, plan, implement, and review seemingly every moment of every day. The Welsh Government (2021 p. 15) committed to not making their latest approach to emotional and mental well-being 'overly bureaucratic'. Making interventions effective without over-loading teachers with additional paperwork can also have the benefit of making us feel that what we do is valued and supported not just measured and assessed. Changing the way we understand things, changing the way we say things, helping in new ways – sometimes more and sometimes less – and developing awareness of self and of others can 'lighten the load'. These changes can mean new feelings of safety, belonging, and space to learn for pupils.

> Issues that affect teacher well-being can have a significant knock-on effect for learner well-being. Emotionally and mentally healthy teachers are better able to develop strong teacher–learner relationships. This in turn is important not simply in terms of ensuring academic attainment, but in fostering an ethos that nurtures the young person, building their cooperation, commitment, resilience and confidence.
> *(Welsh Government, 2021 p. 37)*

Teaching resilience, emotional intelligence, and positive coping strategies arms CYP with the knowledge and skills they can employ as they navigate the obstacles and challenges intrinsic to each stage of development. Supporting better mental health in schools through curriculum provision that:

- develops strategies for emotional containment
- develops cognition of the struggles and inherent psychological challenges of growing up and when that becomes something requiring a more targeted approach

Mental health and the role of schools

- works on improving relationships and connections by developing compassionate listening skills

are ideas in line with the English Government's 2021 eight principles for promoting mental health and well-being for CYP (PHE & DfE, 2021). The eight principles are:

- curriculum teaching and learning to promote resilience and support social and emotional learning
- enabling students' voices to influence decisions
- staff development to support their own well-being and that of students
- identifying needs and monitoring impact of interventions
- working with parents and carers
- targeted support and appropriate referral
- an ethos and environment that promotes respect and values diversity
- leadership and management that supports and champions efforts to promote emotional health and well-being.

The Children's Society's 2020 'Waiting in line' report found a lack of knowledge about their own mental health was cited by young people as a challenge, suggesting that the initiatives to include teaching on mental health in the curriculum in Northern Ireland (CCEA, n.d.), England (DfE, 2019), Scotland (Education Scotland, 2019), and Wales (Welsh Government, 2020a) will be welcomed.

It is important not to see the inherent challenges of growing up as something that needs an intervention from a medical, health, or therapy service (CQC, 2017; Hafal, 2016). Greenberg and Wessely (2017) warn of the frequent tendency to assume vulnerability and not recognise the presence of resilience. Most, but not all, families and children demonstrated resilience during the challenges of the pandemic and, on returning to schools after initial lockdowns, there were soon signs of an improvement in the feelings of CYP about their lives (The Children's Society, 2021). Many of us are more resilient than we realise; we do mostly recover and regain our mental well-being, despite periods of mental health challenges as we grow, develop, and live through the highs and lows of human experience.

> [M]ost of the emotional issues young people and school staff will encounter are not clinical in nature and do not require specialist interventions. Rather, it is about supporting the young person, building their resilience and fostering a sense that there is someone they can trust.
>
> *(Welsh Government, 2021 p. 17)*

Sir Simon Wessely (Greenberg & Wessely, 2017; DfHSC, 2018) confirmed that recovery from immediate challenges, such as loss and unexpected change, experienced by so many, not least during the COVID-19 pandemic and subsequent social limitations, can be best supported through existing relational bonds and everyday community connections. The community in which CYP spend a majority of their time is our community: the community of school.

Some pupils will, at some times, require additional support outside of the school community for their mental well-being. Increased knowledge and understanding can support the development of resilience. The ability to contain our own emotions and those of our pupils can create conditions in which pupils who struggle with emotion regulation can build their skills and strategies for self-regulation. Expression of compassion to pupils and towards ourselves can be 'catching' and make for kinder classrooms. Compassion fosters connection; building connections in schools engenders a sense of belonging which can increase engagement and feelings of purpose and satisfaction with life. There is much we can do to support the everyday fluctuations in the mental health of our pupils and to develop resilience in those in our schools who have not had enough opportunities in previous relationships and environments to build their ability to bounce back.

Responding to the pandemic

The impact of the pandemic and the unprecedented constraints put in place to mitigate the risks of contagion amplified existing concerns about the increase of poor mental health in CYP, alongside the paucity of services primed to respond to the need (Ford et al., 2021). The impact of the pandemic on mental health was seen to be experienced differently across demographics; the age of pupils at the time of lockdowns and their socioeconomic status contributed to variations in outcomes (OECD, 2020; Ford et al., 2021). Adolescents may have been particularly harmed by lack of peer contact and the challenge of managing their own learning time and environment (Holzer et al., 2021). In Northern Ireland, three-quarters of young people surveyed by the Secondary Students' Union of Northern Ireland (SSUNI) (2021) reported experiencing mental health issues during the COVID-19 pandemic. The SSUNI explained that the high incidence reflected a higher baseline of mental health issues in Northern Ireland, known to exist, and were attributed to the ongoing legacy from the Troubles.

While the COVID-19 pandemic potentially increased the need for emotional support in schools, concern over the impact of lockdowns meant that some felt catch-up learning had to take priority over mental well-being. The question as to whether we could 'do it all' – give extra attention to academic learning and to emotional well-being – was a national discussion. Teachers, parents, pupils, and society engaged in the conversation as to what to prioritise in schools to best recover from the impact of the pandemic lockdown. Gavin Williamson (2021), the then Minister for Education in England, prioritised behaviour and discipline over other areas of school provision on the 2021 return to schools. He suggested that expecting students to 'choose' to 'behave well' was the most important way to support the return to school and the recovery for pupils. This could lead to further detriment to those pupils who may be disciplined for behaviours that are symptoms of mental health needs rather than choosing not to 'behave well' (Mind, 2021). The Welsh Government 2020 update to 'Education in Wales: Our national mission' (Welsh Government, 2020b) seemed to put an emphasis on addressing the impact of financial inequalities on learning and on continuing the planned implementation of the new curriculum. In a poll conducted for The Institute for Public Policy Research (IPPR, 2020), almost three-quarters of parents who responded wanted the focus of schools to be on supporting mental health.

The experience of the worldwide COVID-19 pandemic has illustrated how quickly and widely new threats can emerge that jeopardise our experience and feelings of safety and security. Gibson (2022) felt that the experience of the pandemic has introduced CYP to the unpredictability of an uncertain future. Future threats have been emerging for some time. They may not have such a sudden onset and have not had such an immediate and unprecedented response, but there are warnings that we may yet experience a tsunami of poor mental health in our CYP. The most frequently cited emerging risk to the mental health of CYP is climate or eco-anxiety. The 2022 Russian invasion of Ukraine may change this, particularly due to access to so much media coverage of events, and increase worries in CYP about conflicts and war, just as COVID-19 increased their fears about future pandemics.

Preparing for the future

The Royal College of Paediatrics and Child Health (RCPCH) (2021) predicted that by 2040 mental health problems in CYP will pose the greatest risk to our young people and the services that support them. The RCPCH acknowledged the trend was already recognised pre-pandemic. Where and when physical threats, such as further new viruses, will emerge is unknown, but they are anticipated by experts in the field. Our ability to cope with ever-present challenges to our mental well-being, such as loss and change, may be less supported within strained communities, as other stressors, such as inequalities, injustice, social exclusion, and movements of people, continue or increase. The recognition of transgenerational trauma identifies whole other groups whose experiences had not previously been appreciated or addressed (Yehuda & Lehrner, 2018).

The most widely acknowledged impending international crisis is the potential impact of climate change. The existence of global warming and the attendant negative impacts on sea levels, farming, and temperatures in many areas of the world is widely recognised, although exact predictions are not universally agreed. Whatever our feelings about the validity of the predictions from many in the science community, climate change anxiety is a recognised experience, along with eco-anxiety and other names for fears about the future of the planet as we know it.

Young people across the world appear to be engaged in raising awareness and in creating responses to climate change. Research has found that CYP are also the most affected by worry over the future of the planet (Clayton et al., 2020; Hickman, 2020). In the UK, both the main bodies for registered CYP counsellors and psychotherapists acknowledged the need for developing services to respond to this need. In 2019, the United Kingdom Council for Psychotherapists (UKCP) produced an issue of their journal entitled 'Tomorrow's World: Cancelled?' and dedicated their annual conference to the issue. They acknowledged many areas need considering in order to prepare for increasing mental health needs related to the environment. These included recognising the mental health benefits of our relationship with green environments as well as our anxieties around the detriment or disappearance of these very spaces. In 2020, the British Association for Counselling and Psychotherapy's (BACP) commissioned YouGov to undertake a poll to assess the levels of anxiety associated with climate change in the UK. Their findings agreed with other research that CYP are more affected than adults.

In the US, the American Psychological Association (APA) published 'Mental Health and Our Changing Climate: Impacts, Implications, and Guidance' (2017), recognising the growing mental health impacts of climate change on communities dealing with the effects of more frequent damaging weather events. The report also acknowledged the emergence of mental health issues related to climate change and eco-anxiety. CYP may feel anger with the previous generations whom they recognise as the cause of climate change. Involvement in positive action and an ensuing sense of belonging to the activist community may support good mental health, while feeling hopeless or helpless would be detrimental to mental health (Gibson, 2022). For young people and adults having a sense of purpose and of agency are important for mental well-being. Threats to communities can have detrimental effects on mental health, whereas responding to threats as part of a group with a shared purpose can have a positive impact on mental well-being. Recent advice, whether talking about anxieties around current and possible future pandemics, conflicts or economic pressures, includes: practicing kindness or compassion to self as well as others; finding ways to help as part of our compassionate response (APA, 2022; BPS, 2022); and the importance of adults containing and managing their own feelings in order to be able to contain the anxieties of CYP (APA, 2022; BPS, 2022).

Some things may never change. The 2021 Good Childhood Report (The Children's Society, 2021) found that CYP still worry about their exam grades and getting a job after they leave school. They also worry about their own economic well-being as well as wider economic injustices. In addition to the growth of climate change anxiety, unsurprisingly, CYP now worry about possible new diseases (The Children's Society, 2021) and wars (Oxford Health NHS Foundation Trust, 2022). The COVID-19 pandemic may have accelerated an already established trend of increasing mental ill health in the UK and beyond. Services are stretched, and there is a patchwork of expectations, responsibilities, and capacity within health, social care, and education provisions. We in schools are seen as essential mental health responders by society, parents, and pupils. We are doing a good job. We still need time, space, training, budgets, and accessible pathways to specialist services in order to maintain the mental health of pupils and of staff.

Conclusion

Schools are being left to 'pick up the pieces' of inadequate mental health services for CYP (EPI, 2020; LocalGov, 2020; Mind, 2019). Whether we are comfortable with it or not, we are on the frontline of mental health support for our CYP, and in this chapter, we have looked at the need for this support. There are various perceptions about whether it is an integral part of our role, an additional responsibility for which we are or are not valued and acknowledged, or if we are 'picking up the pieces' for other failing services.

The following 2020 statement from the DfE in England suggested that we need to effectively support children's mental health because we should all care about children's well-being but also because children need to feel mentally well if they are going to learn:

> It is important that children and young people have good wellbeing as the hallmark of a caring and just society and it is through children and young people's wellbeing that the conditions are created for their development into their full potential. These values are central to the Department for Education's (DfE) vision to provide world-class education, training, and care for everyone, whatever their background.
>
> *(DfE, 2020 p. 18)*

We are going to be approached or depended on by pupils through their own choices; as a result, we need to be available and informed. Referring every pupil's struggle with their mental health to medical services can cause harm rather than lead to healing. We should not fall into being part of a system that leads to seeing life experiences and the challenges of growing up as things no child or young person is going to manage and that they must, therefore, be addressed through medical pathways and prescriptions. Knowing the specialist services are there, accessible, adaptable, and sufficient when pupils need them would reduce stress for pupils, parents, and teachers. We need more effective ways of identifying need and the level of a need. We need to know what the appropriate response or intervention is for that need and where and when this can be accessed.

We may, at times, feel obliged by society's expectation that we fill the gap in mental health services. With fully functioning health and social care services, accessible as appropriate to the needs of CYP, schools will then offer mental health support that fits within their remit, and that can be evidenced to be effective, happily delivered by staff and valued by pupils. When we ourselves feel our mental health is supported and our role in supporting the mental health of students is recognised and resourced, we can then experience the privilege of being trusted by our students and seen as a person with whom they want to share their challenges.

References

Ahmedani, B. (2011) Mental health stigma: Society, individuals, and the profession. *Journal of Social Work Values and Ethics*, 8 (2), 41–416.

All-Party Parliamentary Group on a Fit and Healthy Childhood (2021) *The Covid Generation: A Mental Health Pandemic in the Making.* Available from: https://fhcappg.org.uk/wp-content/uploads/2021/04/THE-COVID-GENERATION-REPORT-April2021.pdf [Accessed 10th January 2022].

American Psychological Association (APA) (2017) *Mental Health and Our Changing Climate: Impacts, Implications and Guidance.* Washington, DC: ecoAmerica. Available from: https://www.apa.org/news/press/releases/2017/03/mental-health-climate.pdf [Accessed 14th July 2021].

American Psychological Association (APA) (2022) Talking to kids about the war in Ukraine. 7 March. Available from: https://www.apa.org/news/apa/2022/children-teens-war-ukraine [Accessed 25th May 2022].

Bailey, S. & Knightsmith, P. (2017) Fixing CAMHS funding shortage. *Children and Young People Now* 17 January. Available from: https://www.cypnow.co.uk/features/article/fixing-camhs-funding-shortage [accessed 21st May 2022].

Booth, S. (2021) Mental health first aid training for primary schools ditched, government finally admits. *Schools Week*, 30 July. Available from: https://schoolsweek.co.uk/mental-health-first-aid-training-for-primary-schools-ditched-government-finally-admits/ [Accessed 27th December 2021].

British Association for Counselling and Psychotherapy (BACP) (2020) Mental health impact of climate change. 15 October. Available from: https://www.bacp.co.uk/news/news-from-bacp/2020/15-october-mental-health-impact-of-climate-change/ [Accessed 19th November 2021].

British Psychological Society (BPS) (2022) Supporting children to manage anxiety over war, conflict and crises. Online article. 25 February. Available from: https://www.bps.org.uk/news-and-policy/supporting-children-manage-anxiety-over-war-conflict-and-crises [Accessed 25th May 2022].

Care Quality Commission (CQC) (2017) Review of children and young people's mental health services. Available from: https://www.cqc.org.uk/publications/major-report/review-children-young-peoples-mental-health-services-phase-one-report [Accessed 05th October 2021].

Centre for Mental Health (2021) Children and young people's mental health: The facts. Available from: https://www.centreformentalhealth.org.uk/fact-sheet-children-and-young-peoples-mental-health [Accessed 12th September 2021].

Children's Commissioner for England (2020) The state of children's mental health services. Available from: https://www.childrenscommissioner.gov.uk/report/the-state-of-childrens-mental-health-services/ [Accessed 5th October 2021].

Children's Commissioner for Wales (2020) No wrong door: Bringing services together to meet children's needs. Available from: https://www.childcomwales.org.uk/publications/no-wrong-door-bringing-services-together-to-meet-childrens-needs/ [Accessed 19th December 2021].

Clayton, S., Bryan T. and Karazsia, B. (2020) Development and validation of a measure of climate change anxiety. *Journal of Environmental Psychology*, 69. Available from: doi: 10.1016/j.jenvp.2020.101434

Community Children's Health Partnership (CCHP) (2007) Referral guidelines for access to the specialist NHS-based CAMHs teams. Available from: https://cchp.nhs.uk/sites/default/files/filemanager/CCHP/Clinicians/CAMHS/Referral%20Guidelines%20for%20Access%20to%20the%20Specialist%20NHS-Based%20CAMHS%20Teams.pdf [Accessed 12th January 2022].

Corrigan, P. and Watson, A. (2002) Understanding the impact of stigma on people with mental illness. *World Psychiatry: Official Journal of the World Psychiatric Association (WPA)*, 1 (1), 16–20.

Council for the Curriculum, Examinations & Assessment (CCEA) (n.d.) Curriculum aim and objectives: Aim of the Northern Ireland curriculum. Available from: https://ccea.org.uk/about/what-we-do/curriculum/curriculum-aim-and-objectives [Accessed 12th January 2022].

Danby, G. and Hamilton, P. (2016) Addressing the 'elephant in the room'. The role of the primary school practitioner in supporting children's mental well-being. *Pastoral Care in Education*, 34 (2), 90–103.

Deighton, J., Lereya, S., Casey, P., Patalay, P., Humphrey, N. and Wolpert, M. (2019) Prevalence of mental health problems in schools: Poverty and other risk factors among 28,000 adolescents in England. *British Journal of Psychiatry*, 215 (3), 565–567.

Department for Children, Schools and Families (DCSF) (2008) *Targeted Mental Health in Schools Project. Using the Evidence to Inform Your Approach: A Practical Guide for Headteachers and Commissioners*. Nottingham: DCSF Publications.

Department for Education (DfE) (2017) Mental health and schools link pilot: Evaluation. Available from: https://www.gov.uk/government/publications/mental-health-services-and-schools-link-pilot-evaluation [Accessed 19th December 2021]. Open Government Licence v1.0. OGL. Full details available from: https://www.nationalarchives.gov.uk/doc/open-government-licence/version/3/.

Department for Education (DfE) (2019) All pupils will be taught about mental and physical wellbeing. Press Release 25 February. Available from: https://www.gov.uk/government/news/all-pupils-will-be-taught-about-mental-and-physical-wellbeing [Accessed 24th November 2021].

Department for Education (DfE) (2020) State of the nation 2020: Children and young people's wellbeing: Research report. Available from: https://www.gov.uk/government/publications/state-of-the-nation-2020-children-and-young-peoples-wellbeing [Accessed 30th November 2021].

Department of Health (2015) Future in mind: Promoting, protecting and improving our children and young people's mental health and wellbeing. Available from: https://assets.publishing.service.gov.uk/government/uploads/system/uploads/attachment_data/file/414024/Childrens_Mental_Health.pdf [Accessed 28th August 2021].

Department of Health and Social Care (DfHSC) (2018) Modernising the mental health act: Final report from the independent review. Available from: https://www.gov.uk/government/publications/modernising-the-mental-health-act-final-report-from-the-independent-review [Accessed 17th July 2021].

Department of Health and Social Care and Department for Education (DoHSC) (DfE) (2017) *Transforming Children and Young People's Mental Health Provision: A Green Paper*. London: Crown Copyright.

Education Policy Unit (EPI) (2020) Access to child and adolescent mental health services in 2019. Available from: https://epi.org.uk/publications-and-research/access-to-child-and-adolescent-mental-health-services-in-2019/ [Accessed 28th August 2021].

Education Scotland (2019) Curriculum for excellence. Available from: https://education.gov.scot/Documents/All-experiencesoutcomes18.pdf [Accessed 30th September 2021].

Finning, K., White, J., Toth, K., Golden, S., MelendezTorres, G. and Ford, T. (2021) Longerterm effects of schoolbased counselling in UK primary schools. *European Child & Adolescent Psychiatry*. [online] Available from: doi: 10.1007/s00787-021-01802-w

Ford, T., John, A. and Gunnell, D. (2021) Mental health of children and young people during pandemic. *BMJ* 372 (614) [online]. Available from: doi: 10.1136/bmj.n614

Gibson, K. (2022) *What Young People Want from Mental Health Services: A Youth Informed Approach for the Digital Age*. Abingdon, Oxon: Routledge.

Gordon, J. and Platt, S. (2017) *Going to Be All Right? A Report on the Mental Health of Young People in Scotland*. Glasgow: SAMH.

Gov. UK (2017) Secondary school staff get mental health 'first aid' training. 27 June. Available from: https://www.gov.uk/government/news/secondary-school-staff-get-mental-health-first -aid-training [Accessed 21st October 2021].

Greenberg, N. and Wessely, S. (2017) Mental health interventions for people involved in disasters: What not to do. *World Psychiatry*, 16 (3), 249–250.

Hafal (2016) Making sense: A report by young people on their well-being and mental health. Available from: https://www.hafal.org/wp-content/uploads/2018/07/A-report-by-young -people-on-their-well-being-and-mental-health.pdf [Accessed 9th November 2021].

Hickman, C. (2020) We need to (find a way to) talk about … eco-anxiety. *Journal of Social Work Practice*, 34 (4), 411–424.

Hobby, R. (2017) Teachers are constantly forced to fill the void as the gaps in children's mental health services grow. *Times Educational Supplement (TES)* 11 January. Available from: https://www.tes.com/news/teachers-are-constantly-forced-fill-void-gaps-childrens-mental -health-services-grow [Accessed 16th October 2021].

Holzer, J., Lüftenegger, M., Käser, U., Korlat, S., Pelikan, E., Schultze-Krumbholz, A., Spiel, C., Wachs, S. and Scober, B. (2021) Students' basic needs and well-being during the COVID-19 pandemic: A two-country study of basic psychological need satisfaction, intrinsic learning motivation, positive emotion and the moderating role of self-regulated learning. *International Journal of Psychology*, 56 (6), 843–852.

House of Commons (2018) The Government's Green Paper on mental health: 'Failing a generation'. Available from: https://dera.ioe.ac.uk//31764/ [Accessed 08th August 2021].

House of Commons Education and Health Committees (2017) Children and young people's mental health – the role of education, First Joint Report of Session 2016–17, HC 849. Available from: https://www.publications.parliament.uk/pa/cm201617/cmselect/cmhealth /849/849.pdf [Accessed 26th September 2021].

Institute for Public Policy Research (IPPR) (2020) Making the vulnerable visible: Narrowing the attainment gap after Covid-19. Available from: https://www.ippr.org/blog/making-the -vulnerable-visible [Accessed 16th January 2022].

Kidger, J., Turner, N., Hollingworth, W., Evans, R., Bell, S., Brockman, R., Copeland, L., Fisher, H., Harding, S., Powell, J., Araya, R., Campell, R., Ford, T., Gunnel, D., Murphy, S. and Morris, R. (2021) An intervention to improve teacher well-being support and training to support students in UK high schools (the WISE study): A cluster randomised controlled trial. *PLoS Medicine*, 18 (11). Available from: doi: 10.1371/journal.pmed.1003847

Lavis, P., Burke, C. and Hastings, R. (2019) Overshadowed: The mental health needs of children and young people with learning disabilities. The Children and Young People's Mental Health Coalition. Available from: https://cypmhc.org.uk/publications/overshadowed/ [Accessed 23rd August 2021].

LocalGov (2020) Councils and teachers call for over £5bn of extra school funding. 5 March. Available from: https://www.localgov.co.uk/Councils-and-teachers-call-for-over-5bn-of -extra-school-funding-/50126 [Accessed 31st August 2021].

Mansfield, R., Humphrey, N. and Patalay, P. (2021) Educators' perceived mental health literacy and capacity to support students' mental health: associations with school-level characteristics and provision in England. *Health Promotion International*, 1–12. Available from: doi: 10.1093/heapro/daab010. Creative Commons CC BY license. Full details available at: https:// creativecommons.org/licenses/by/4.0/.

Mental Health Foundation (2016) Mental health in Wales: Fundamental facts 2016. Available from: https://www.mentalhealth.org.uk/wales [Accessed 14th September].

Mental Health Foundation (2017) Welsh assembly children, young people and education committee: The first 1000 days. Available from: https://www.mentalhealth.org.uk/sites/default/files/1702_MHF_response_CYPE%20Committee_First%201000%20days_0.pdf [Accessed 12th November 2021].

Mental Health Foundation (2019) State of a generation: Preventing mental health problems in children and young people. Available from: https://www.mentalhealth.org.uk/publications/state-generation-preventing-mental-health-problems-children-and-young-people [Accessed 17th October 2021].

Mental Health Foundation (2021) Stigma and discrimination. 04th October. Available from: https://www.mentalhealth.org.uk/a-to-z/s/stigma-and-discrimination [Accessed 22nd January 2022].

Mental Health Foundation (n.d.) 70% of Scotland's teachers lack training to address mental health problems in schools. Available from: https://www.mentalhealth.org.uk/news/70-scotlands-teachers-lack-training-address-mental-health-problems-schools [Accessed 22nd December 2021].

Mind (2019) Three in five young people have experienced a mental health problem or are close to someone who has. 2 July. Available from: https://www.mind.org.uk/news-campaigns/news/three-in-five-young-people-have-experienced-a-mental-health-problem-or-are-close-to-someone-who-has/ [Accessed 24th September 2021].

Mind (2021) Not making the grade: Why our approach to mental health at secondary school is failing young people. Available from: https://www.mind.org.uk/news-campaigns/campaigns/children-and-young-peoples-mental-health/improving-mental-health-support-for-young-people/#problem [Accessed 16th January 2022].

National Assembly for Wales (NAW) Children, Young People and Education Committee (2018) Mind over matter: A report on the step change needed in emotional and mental health support for children and young people in Wales. Available from: https://senedd.wales/laid%20documents/cr-ld11522/cr-ld11522-e.pdf [Accessed 16th January 2022]. Open Government licence v3.0. OGL. Full details available from: https://www.nationalarchives.gov.uk/doc/open-government-licence/version/3/.

National Education Union (NEU) (2019) The state of education: Young people's mental health. 17 April. Available from: https://neu.org.uk/press-releases/state-education-young-peoples-mental-health [Accessed 16th January 2022].

NHS Digital (2020) Mental health of children and young people in England 2020, wave 1 follow-up to the 2017 survey. Available from: https://digital.nhs.uk/data-and-information/publications/statistical/mental-health-of-children-and-young-people-in-england/2020-wave-1-follow-up [Accessed 25th July 2021]. Information from NHS Digital, licenced under the current version of the Open Government Licence.

NHS Digital (2021) Health of children and young people in England, 2021 wave 2 follow up to the 2017 survey. Available from: https://digital.nhs.uk/data-and-information/publications/statistical/mental-health-of-children-and-young-people-in-england/2021-follow-up-to-the-2017-survey [Accessed 9th November 2021]. Information from NHS Digital, licenced under the current version of the Open Government Licence.

North Wales Social Care and Well-being Improvement Collaborative (2017) North Wales population assessment. Available from: https://www.denbighshire.gov.uk/en/documents/your-council/statistics-and-data/north-wales-population-assessment/full-report.pdf [Accessed 16th January 2022].

Northern Ireland Direct (n.d.) Independent Counselling Service for schools. Available from: https://www.nidirect.gov.uk/articles/independent-counselling-service-schools [Accessed 8th November 2021].

Organisation for Economic Co-operation and Development (OECD) (2020) The impact of COVID-19 on student equity and inclusion: Supporting vulnerable students during school closures and school re-openings. 19 November. Available from: https://www.oecd.org/coronavirus/policy-responses/the-impact-of-covid-19-on-student-equity-and-inclusion

Mental health and the role of schools

-supporting-vulnerable-students-during-school-closures-and-school-re-openings-d593b5c8/ [Accessed 12th January 2022].

Oxford Health NHS Foundation Trust (2022) Worrying about war in Ukraine: Anxiety and wellbeing advice for you and your family. 16 March. Available at: https://www.oxfordhealth .nhs.uk/news/taking-simple-steps-to-ease-worries-and-support-others/ [Accessed 25th May 2022].

Pattison, S., Robson, M., Hunt, K. and Dacre, V. (2011) Evaluation of the Welsh School-based counselling primary pilot: Final report. December. Available from: https://citeseerx.ist.psu.edu /viewdoc/download?doi=10.1.1.456.3638&rep=rep1&type=pdf [Accessed 19th December 2021].

Pells, R. (2017) Four-year-olds suffering panic attacks, eating disorders, anxiety and depression, report says. *The Independent.* Available from: https://www.independent.co.uk/news/ education/education-news/uk-schools-mental-health-surge-support-issues-children-pupils -nasuwt-barnardos-a7 82751.html [Accessed 19th December 2021].

Public Health England (2016) *The Mental Health of Children and Young People in England.* London: Public Health England. Available from: https://assets.publishing.service.gov.uk /government/uploads/system/uploads/attachment_data/file/575632/Mental_health_of_ children_in_England.pdf [Accessed 16th December 2021].

Public Health England (PHE) and Department for Education (DfE) (2021) Promoting children and young people's mental health and wellbeing: A whole school or college approach. Available from: https://www.gov.uk/government/publications/promoting-children-and-young -peoples-emotional-health-and-wellbeing [Accessed 23rd January 2022]. Open Government Licence v3.0. OGL. Full details available at: https://www.nationalarchives.gov.uk/doc/open -government-licence/version/3/

Rocks S., Fazel M. and Tsiachristas, A. (2020) Impact of transforming mental health services for young people in England on patient access, resource use and health: A quasi-experimental study. *BMJ Open.* 10, e034067, Available from: doi: 10.1136/bmjopen-2019-034067

Royal College of Paediatrics and Child Health (RCPCH) (2021) Paediatrics 2040 forecasting the future. Available from: https://paediatrics2040.rcpch.ac.uk/ [Accessed 23rd January 2022].

Scottish Government (2020) Guidance for education authorities establishing access to counselling in secondary schools. Available from: https://www.gov.scot/publications/guidance-education -authorities-establishing-access-counselling-secondary-schools/ [Accessed 12th July 2021].

Secondary Students' Union of Northern Ireland (SSUNI) (2021) Mental health matters: Secondary school mental health reform in NI: A report on mental health and education in the COVID pandemic. Available from: https://ssuni.org/mentalhealth [Accessed 12th July 2021].

Shelemy, L., Harvey, K. and Waite, P. (2019) Secondary school teachers' experiences of supporting mental health. *Journal of Mental Health Training, Education and Practice*, 14 (5), 372–383.

Soneson, E. and Ford, T. (2020) Identifying mental health difficulties in children & young people: The role of schools. Available from: https://www.acamh.org/blog/identifying-mental-health -difficulties-in-children-young-people-the-role-of-schools/ [Accessed 21st August 2021].

Taylor, C. (2016) *Review of the Youth Justice System in England and Wales.* London: Ministry of Justice. Available from: https://www.gov.uk/government/publications/review-of-the-youth -justice-system [Accessed 12th January 2022].

The Children's Society (2020) Waiting in line: Stories of young people accessing mental health support. Available from: https://www.childrenssociety.org.uk/information/professionals/ resources/waiting-line [Accessed 19th December 2021].

The Children's Society (2021) The good childhood report 2021. Available from: https://www .childrenssociety.org.uk/information/professionals/resources/good-childhood-report-2021 [Accessed 23rd January 2022].

UK Parliament (2021) Provision of school-based counselling services. *Research Briefing.* 5 November. Available from: https://commonslibrary.parliament.uk/research-briefings/cdp -2021-0178/ [Accessed 08th December 2021]. Open Parliament Licence v3.0. OPL. Full details available from: https://www.parliament.uk/site-information/copyright-parliament/open-parliament-licence/.

United Kingdom Council for Psychotherapists (UKCP) (2019) Tomorrow's world: Cancelled? *New Psychotherapist*, 72(Autumn) online. Available from: https://www.psychotherapy.org.uk/newpsychotherapist/?SortBy=Newest%20first [Accessed 19th July 2021].

Welsh Assembly Government (2008) *School-Based Counselling Services in Wales*. Cardiff: WAG.

Welsh Government (2020a) A new curriculum in Wales: Changing the way children and young people learn in school. Available from: https://hwb.gov.wales/curriculum-for-wales/a-new-curriculum-in-wales-easy-read/ [Accessed 11th June 2021].

Welsh Government (2020b) Education in Wales: Our national mission update October 2021. Available from: https://gov.wales/education-wales-our-national-mission-update-october-2020-html [Accessed 11th June 2021].

Welsh Government (2020c) Review of evidence on all-age mental health services: Summary. Available from: https://gov.wales/sites/default/files/statistics-and-research/2020-06/review-of-evidence-on-all-age-mental-health-services-summary.pdf [Accessed 11th June 2021]. Open Government Licence v3.0. OGL. Full details available at: https://www.nationalarchives.gov.uk/doc/open-government-licence/version/3/

Welsh Government (2021) Framework guidance on embedding a whole-school approach to mental health and wellbeing. Available from: https://gov.wales/sites/default/files/publications/2021-03/framework-on-embedding-a-whole-school-approach-to-emotional-and-mental-well-being.pdf [Accessed 19th December 2021] Open Government Licence v3.0. OGL. Full details available from: https://www.nationalarchives.gov.uk/doc/open-government-licence/version/3/

Williamson, G. (2021) Education secretary speech to FED national education summit. 1 March. Available from: https://www.gov.uk/government/speeches/education-secretary-speech-to-fed-national-education-summit [Accessed 19th January 2022].

Yehuda, R. and Lehrner, A. (2018) Intergenerational transmission of trauma effects: Putative role of epigenetic mechanisms. *World Psychiatry: Official Journal of the World Psychiatric Association (WPA)*, 17 (3), 243–257. Available from: doi.org/10.1002/wps.20568

YMCA (2016) *I Am Whole: A Report Investigating the Stigma Faced by Young People Experiencing Mental Health Difficulties*. London: YMCA.

Young Minds (2019) Lack of early support for young people's mental health puts pressure on GPs. 7 November. Available from: https://www.youngminds.org.uk/about-us/media-centre/press-releases/lack-of-early-support-for-young-people-s-mental-health-puts-pressure-on-gps/ [Accessed 17th May 2021].

Chapter 2

Cognition

What is cognition?

For the purpose of this book, and this chapter in particular, cognition means thought processes, the knowledge, understanding and the 'thinking about' and the 'learning about' we engage in for our professional life. Knowing and understanding ourselves, and who and how we are in all areas of our lives, enhances our ability to teach and to relate to pupils.

Cognition is at the heart of education provision in schools. Cognition encompasses how we perceive, remember, assess, imagine, create, and resolve (APA Dictionary of Psychology, n.d.). In other words, cognition is making sense of the world, holding onto that sense, and using that sense to navigate life; so, it's pretty essential all-in-all. Through cognition, we piece together and remember incoming information from environments and relationships, and we are aware of and remember things about our internal lives. Knowledge of our thought processes may lead to new understanding. If we are aware that we have a certain pattern of cognition, and that, in order to make sense of our lives, we create templates and maps for navigating and predicting our world, it is more likely that we will see that these patterns are unique to us, built by our own experiences and our interpretation of those experiences.

Theory of mind – the ability to understand or think about the minds of others, to know that others experience thoughts like we do, and to guess, imagine or understand the thoughts of another – is important cognition for our social engagement. Around age four to five, children are realising that others have thoughts of their own and that their own thoughts (assumptions and beliefs) may not always be right. This is an ongoing challenge in life; accepting that our own thoughts and beliefs may not represent objective realities may feel challenging to our sense of self and of security, but it is essential to social integration. Social cognition develops as we mature and increases our abilities to communicate, compromise, agree to disagree, and recognise, hopefully with respect, differences in thoughts and beliefs. Sometimes it feels more comfortable to be aware of the thoughts of others than it does to look more closely at ways that we think or notice how what we believe impacts ourselves and others. Fostering a habit of examining our own mental states, our perception, belief, desire, and intention primes us for thinking about others' state of mind, developing our theory of mind (Böckler et al., 2017).

DOI: 10.4324/9781003277903-3

Cognition

Peter Fonagy (Bateman & Fonagy, 2013; Fonagy, 2008; Fonagy & Allison, 2012) described the ability to consider our and others' thoughts as mentalisation. Mentalisation is a cognitive way of understanding. Mentalisation is our endeavour to conceive of our own state of mind and thoughts and those of others (Halfon et al., 2017). Accurate perceptions of the motivations of others forms part of mentalisation, tempered by an understanding that we cannot know this with complete certainty. Understanding the experience of others is often a felt understanding: empathy is the emotional understanding of another's experience and mentalisation is a cognitive way of understanding others. As we experience thoughts and feelings, we may notice that we are thinking about the thoughts and the feelings, making sense of them or just being aware they are there. Swan and Riley (2015) believed that the ability to feel and think about our feelings leads to an ability to accept our responsibility for our actions. Having cognition of how we feel and think and then act gives us choices and allows for informed reflection and the possibility of change.

Simon Borg (2003) conducted a review of literature on teacher cognition. Borg recognised the impact of teacher cognition, the influence of their mental states, and their cognitive ways of processing on their professional practice. The review considered how resistant to change our cognitions – what we think, know, or believe – can be. This gives us cause to think this is likely true for our pupils as well. As educators, we are in the business of changing minds. Change may not come easily; it will need time and is facilitated or enabled by teachers rather than compelled or imposed (Zull, 2002). Zull explained that we teachers cannot rewire a pupil's brain, but we are in the business of creating environments and relationships that support cognitive growth and adaptation. Nelson et al. (2015) believed that professional development, continuing change in our understanding, takes time, needs ongoing support, and is best developed in relationships with colleagues and with external consultants. We can change, as can our pupils, but it takes time, patience, perseverance, and support.

Why does cognition matter for teachers' practice?

Educating children and young people (CYP) is a privilege for us as educators and a vital service for individuals, communities, and the future of everyone. We need to, and do, shoulder our responsibility and accountability in doing a great job in a great way. A series of books, 'Why do teachers need to know about…', explores what it is that teachers need to know and understand in order to inform their practice. One book in the series considers the subject of psychological understanding (Monsen et al., 2021) and another the understanding of developmental needs (Maisey & Campbell-Barr, 2021). Our professional responsibility is to know what we need to know in order to be accountable and proficient in the privileged role we chose, love, and have full commitment to. Husbands and Pearce (2012) agreed that what we know, do, and believe underpin successful pedagogy. It is also important to know what we do not know and when we need to learn more. Knowing what we do not know makes us better and safer practitioners.

Professional requirements, the standards expected of us, include that we have cognitive awareness of evolving knowledge and understanding of how we teach and why we teach (DfE, 2019; Ofsted, 2019; Perry et al., 2021). The DfE (2019) professional standards stress the importance of cognitive science in the knowledge of how children learn. Social cognition, the way we understand, think about, process, and respond to others (Blakemore & Frith, 2005), underpins classroom dynamics and teacher behaviours, but awareness of it is not yet recognised to be of equal value in the teaching profession to the mechanics of subject teaching and learning. Paying attention to other areas of cognition, such as cognitive psychodynamics (Horowitz, 1998), relationship intelligence (Wascher et al., 2018), and the cognitive processes which drive our responses to others, really matter to emotional well-being and better mental health in schools. They also matter for academic achievement. Cognition of psychological and developmental needs are as necessary to good pedagogy as cognition of how pupils take in, store, and retrieve information.

In order to understand from a different perspective, for instance, to see an event as a pupil may see it, we need to be open to different interpretations and beliefs. This is more likely if we are aware of our own perspectives and beliefs about life and relationships. When we know and understand that there are different interpretations, beliefs, perspectives, ways of seeing, and ways of experiencing events and interactions, we feel less threatened or less confused by the ways others construct their reality. Feeling open, curious, and able to tolerate challenge and difference allows us to experience and demonstrate compassion, provide containment, and build connection to others.

We do not need to know a child's history to believe that, whatever the narrative of their life story, it will inform their perceptions, understandings, and beliefs. This, in turn, impacts how children make sense of cause and effect and their perceptions and predictions of people's positive or negative attributions to them. The behaviours, attitudes, and beliefs we observe in our more vulnerable or seemingly challenging pupils are all expressions of the physical brain created by the child's efforts to survive (Zull, 2002). When we hold this in mind and try not to attribute pupil behaviours to 'attention seeking', laziness, or obstructiveness, we can consider whether the behaviours indicate missing skill sets, unmet needs, or that responses appropriate to previous experiences are informing current situations. Curiosity and openness to possibilities in understanding others lead to potential for creating more effective responses and problem-solving ideas. It also changes our feelings about the intentions that may be directing the behaviour. With this in mind, we can reframe our thoughts and see the behaviours as child-directed safety and preservation serving rather than teacher-directed attacks. This, in turn, reduces feelings of being targeted, undermined, or personally disliked, alleviating teacher stress and emotional exhaustion. Removing barriers of misunderstanding and misattribution makes more space for connection. Attachment theory suggests a framework for why early relationships shape why we behave as we do, why others' behaviours make us feel as they do, and why we react to others, to situations and to relationships, as we do. Knowledge of motivation and mental states in both ourselves and others can underpin the ways we select how to improve environments, enhance positive experiences, and use relational skills as best fitting to situations and pupil needs.

Knowledge and understanding changes feelings and beliefs. When we understand cause and effect in our world and have knowledge that helps us predict outcomes, our feelings of safety are increased. This again changes our emotional state. When we can normalise feelings and reactions in terms of neurobiology and the condition of being human, our ability to feel compassion grows. This could be compassion for self or compassion for others.

People cannot know what they have not had opportunity to know (Frith & Frith, 2006). A pupil may not know something we expect them to know because they have not experienced things that we assume are basic human experiences. To know safety is based on having experienced, or at least having seen, safety. To know respect, care, predictable cause and effect, and many other tenets underpinning our classroom ethos means having experienced those circumstances. When we are cognisant of this reality,

Cognition

we become more compassionate of behaviours that we see because they may be, in reality, based on lack of knowledge or skills rather than being a choice to not comply or behave as requested.

Understanding the causes underlying the behaviours of pupils

Eamon McRory (2021), an expert in trauma, explained that the *one* thing he would wish for school staff that would have the biggest beneficial impact on CYP mental health would be to understand the reasons behind pupil behaviours. McCrory believed that if we can reframe the behaviours we see in terms of underlying fear, trauma, anxiety, and mistrust, we would respond more helpfully. Pupils have also reported how helpful this shift in teacher understanding would be for their experience of school as an inclusive, safe, and just environment (The Children's Society, 2021).

Lew and Bettner (1998) believed, like McCrory, that if we understand the underlying motivation for behaviours, we will understand the needs of the student and how their behaviours often belie those needs. Kourkoutasa and Giovazolias (2015) described that what we hear and see in pupil's behaviours tells us their life stories and that we react to the symptoms and behaviours rather than the cause, the underlying experiences. Understanding that behaviours can be symptoms of experiences that are similar to the here and now helps us to try and interpret how things may be perceived through a cloudy or distorting lens. Whether pupils challenge or conform, are hard to manage or easy to miss, they may be behaving *'as if'* the situation is something they recognise, rather than responding to the situation as it is. Dreikurs et al. (1971) call this 'mistaken goals of behaviour'; complying in order to be safe when the situation holds no danger, or fading into the background to avoid being criticised when the other person actually seeks to support and encourage.

We often react to the behaviours of pupils rather than responding to the need the behaviours may be communicating. Mistaken or short-term goals of behaviour may present as seeking attention, power, or revenge or as avoidance (Dreikurs et al., 1971). In responding, we could be more helpful to pupils if we take on board the idea of 'The Crucial Cs', which are four things every human requires, particularly in childhood. Each starts with a C: connect, capable, count, and courage (Lew, 2002; Saxner, 2021). When we find a way to demonstrate the message 'I hold you in mind' to a child who appears to be seeking attention, it could be more productive than dismissing or punishing their need to feel that they matter.

When we feel that we are being challenged or rejected by our students, taking a pause to reflect on what the student may be needing is helpful, to them and to us. Reflecting on how those behaviours might be unconscious efforts to:

- get a need met
- defend against admitting a need,

or the response to experiencing the feelings an unmet need causes can inform our understanding and shape our response.

For example, Stevie needs connection, so he may:

- act in ways that help him connect with peers, sometimes inappropriately
- act in ways that gain adult attention, albeit negative action and attention

- act in ways that ensure his disconnection; to avoid being disconnected by others, he disconnects himself first.

Jessie needs to feel capable, so she may:

- act in ways that demonstrate that she 'can do'; although these are negative actions, they are in her control
- act in ways that avoid taking the risk of feeling incapable; she does not engage, try, or compete
- act in ways that elicit help, ensuring success.

Jamal needs to feel that he counts, so he may:

- act in ways that elicit praise for achievements or behaviours
- act in ways that avoid relationships with adults that he feels do not value his skills
- act in ways that gain positive attention despite diminishing his own sense of comfort or delight.

Delyth needs to feel courage, so she may:

- act in ways that avoid feeling fear or anxiety; she may give up, refuse to take risks, and avoid new experiences
- act in ways that avoid feelings of inferiority; she may refuse to compete or align herself with other students with struggles
- act in ways that are dangerous and take uncalculated risks.

In the model of mistaken goals of behaviour (Dreikurs et al., 1971), students' actions and behaviours are about meeting their own needs not about making teachers' lives difficult. The UK Trauma Council (2020) acknowledged how difficult it can be for school staff not to feel:

- rejected
- pushed away
- angry
- guilty

by 'externalising' or seemingly challenging behaviours.
    We could also feel:

- flattered
- pulled in
- affirmed
- happy

when pupils' behaviours are compliant or pleasing. These are the behaviours we may be least able to notice or question. They may signal pupils have adapted their behaviours to keep themselves safe in ways that then limit their chances of developing their unique potential and good mental health. If behaviours are not challenging to others, they may not be seen as potentially challenging to the rounded development of the individual.

Cognition

When we know and accept that early trauma influences brain development, we may become more open to reflecting on the psychodynamic nature of relationships.

When we reflect on behaviours in terms of the child's previous experiences, their ongoing home context, or feelings about school, learning or peers, we can respond to the behaviour in the context of underlying feelings and be the person who gives space and time for the child to start to process their world. The UK Trauma Council (2020) explained that this can provide opportunities for piecing together new understandings of confusing social experiences. Understanding, or the verbal or non-verbal communication of understanding, is a powerful tool in supporting mental health in everyday interactions. Feeling understood is often an instantaneous de-stressor, helping people to think:

- *If someone else can understand me, I must be understandable.*
- *I am not without sense or reason.*

Feeling that someone understands how your brain works gives the sense of 'they get me'. When this is accompanied by acceptance, and is not about judging, not only can we feel known, but we also experience tolerance and can then imagine that we are not so different that we are unfathomable. This experience is essential before we can then go on to try to understand others.

Responding to seemingly challenging behaviours is not easy. When we know the behaviour may not be personal, it is not only about the 'here and now' or the 'you and me', and our feelings about the behaviour can change. When we are less defensive, we can then give space, time, and maybe personalised strategies to a young person. Openness and curiosity give an opportunity to help pupils explore what they are feeling and why. Teachers who are trained, educated, and supported to understand their own psychodynamic development of cognitions may notice how they can be triggered into responding 'as if' they are facing past experiences. Being aware when responses may be about other times and other places means we may become freed up to create new ways of managing what day-to-day classroom challenges present to us (Kourkoutasa & Giovazolias, 2015).

Understanding the causes underlying the behaviours of teachers

Insight into the needs that may lie behind behaviour and how beliefs about the world are developed through experiences is a cognitive process through which we can develop self-awareness as well as understanding of others. Mentalisation helps us to see pupils' impact on us and our impact on pupils. As we are thinking, we note our thoughts and recognise any feelings associated with them. Thinking about our feelings as we experience them can be a learning opportunity; emotions are helpful because they inform us about our needs, wishes and beliefs. In 2015, Kourkoutas and Giovazolias worked with focus groups of school staff and found that staff working with students are often unaware of the impact students and their behaviours can have on them. They noted that those teachers with more self-awareness were more likely to have a realistic understanding of the impact of students on their feelings and behaviours. Self-aware teachers may see how pupils' needs, emotions, and behaviours lead them to experience strong feelings and to react in certain ways that are not always helpful. It is easy to imagine how these interactions, if not noticed, reflected on, and adapted, can become a negative cycle of distrust, dislike, and stress on both sides.

Philip Riley wrote a groundbreaking book in 2010 reflecting on some of the reasons we may choose to teach. His template is similar to that of Lew and Bettner for pupils (1998) in that he gives language to a set of needs that school staff may not be conscious of but that may drive why they work as teachers and influence how they work in their teaching role. Understanding why we choose to work in schools is likely to make us more helpful to students. Without awareness of why we do what we do, we are unable to consider how our actions feed our own needs or ignore the needs of others.

Riley (2010) directly linked his teacher 'types' to attachment styles. Attachment is understood by many to influence the way we think and feel. Attachment is sometimes called a template for understanding the world. The emotional bond in early life between a baby and carer(s) has an influence on the developing child's emotions and behaviours. The life-long effects and 'playing out' of primary attachment relationships is also often recognised (Gerhardt, 2004; Howe, 2011; Vollman et al., 2019). Our early attachment experiences, the extent to which we felt safe and loved, is a large part of the person we become in adulthood. It is a driver of what we seek or avoid in adult relationships. This may influence the type of work that we choose (Riley, 2010). Having 'good enough' experiences of care early in life leads to feelings of security in later years. Poor care, disrupted care, and care from adults who themselves did not have safe, loving relationships in childhood, or subsequent reparative relationships, lead to feelings of insecurity in later years. These experiences, and our resulting beliefs and ways of being in the world, will naturally have consequences for others we live and work with. Riley's (2010) work informed teachers about possible motivations and unrecognised thought patterns that influence their relationships and work practices, and this may offer opportunities for change that can reduce teacher stress and increase pupil well-being. Teaching has many relational elements, including dynamics such as having a powerful position over others, being helpful, feeling needed, and being liked. It is worthwhile to reflect on our choice of career in light of our emotional needs in order to maintain professional insight and practice.

Our need to protect or provide for others or our unconscious habit of providing or protecting need to be available to our awareness and used in the right doses. Children's need for protection will change with age or developmental stage. But sometimes, we protect children or give them the message they need protecting because we need the feeling this gives us. Denying children risk-taking experiences, chances for feeling that they are brave, and a sense they can become independent of us is detrimental to their growth. Some children have, or have had, such challenging home lives that they elicit our need to provide for their needs. Once we question whether we are meeting their needs or our own need to make things better, we will provide for them in the right doses and not develop relationships that are not appropriate for our education role.

The teacher–pupil relationship can be described as a type of attachment, sometimes referred to as an 'allo' or 'para' attachment. Verschueren and Koomen (2012) described an attachment-like bond with a teacher as 'ad-hoc' and saw it fulfilling two essential attachment functions for pupils: teacher as both a safe haven to turn to and a secure base from which to launch into the world. As humans grow and develop, we need two things from attachment figures:

- a relationship in which the adult is comfortable to support growing autonomy and a child moving away from them with increasing confidence
- a relationship in which the adult is comfortable providing soothing and support when the world gets to be too much (Kerns et al., 2015; Marvin et al., 2002).

Cognition

Insecure children have experienced too much, or too little, of carers being comfortable with letting them go, and they either independently rely on themselves or feel incapable and overly dependent on others. Other insecure children have not had enough of being welcomed back and may not see a parent or carer or us as a secure base to return to.

Kesner (2000) recognised the role of attachment experiences in shaping teacher characteristics, adding that other influences play a part, too. As well as early attachment, Kesner acknowledged that similarities and differences between pupil and teacher can impact relationship building. Later relationships in a teacher's life impact their social and emotional development and ability to relate to others (Kesner, 2000). For us, as for our pupils, there are later chances for building a more secure sense of relationships and more optimism and hope about our relationship with the world or the world with us. Experiencing healthy, appropriate, and positive attachment-like relationships outside of early family bonds can support change in beliefs and in connections in the brain.

Adults and pupils bring their own histories to bear in building relationships in schools. As adults, we are responsible for the quality of those relationships. When we recognise our own relationship style, we have more capacity to keep pupils and ourselves safe and well. Each of us will have our own strengths within relationships and be more comfortable when responding to pupils who need us or with those who appear to deny any need for us. Recognising this in ourselves makes us safer practitioners and offers opportunities for change and growth. Teachers (almost universally) are good enough: great at some things, not so great at others, but certainly good enough. Knowing our strengths and struggles is part of being good enough and of working on being and doing better.

Children may often expect from us what they received from others, and it is more than easy to 'fall into' patterns of relating that are familiar to them or comfortable for us:

- *People hate me; my teacher will hate me.*
- *They think I can't help; I never feel like I can do anything that makes a difference.*

Reflecting on a pupil's behaviour in terms of their needs and their beliefs about us offers opportunities for shifting our responses from ones which keep ourselves and our pupils stuck in familiar, unhelpful patterns of relating in the world to ones which are about building better relationships that can support better mental health for adults and CYP alike in our classrooms and schools.

Cognitive approaches to better mental health in pupils

Cognition is one of the principles for practice we employ to provide environments that support better mental health in schools. We use understanding and knowledge to include ways of working that enhance mental well-being. We include cognitive content in our provisions that offer pupils knowledge and understanding that can help them understand why they feel the way that they do. For some of us, our preferred or more natural way of meeting challenges and connecting in relationship is through cognitive approaches. For some pupils, for various reasons, cognitive approaches to improving mental health are accessible, meaningful, and less threatening than other ways.

Loan your adult brain

Mental state talk is the verbal expression that attributes feelings or thoughts to the actions of ourselves or others. Parents use mental state talk to scaffold their child's understanding of the link between mental states and behaviour (Tomkins et al., 2018). Teachers also use mental state talk to support pupil's understanding of this link (Blackard, 2012). They do this more often and have bigger positive effects on the pupil's development of theory of mind than parents (Wu et al., 2021).

We all like to make sense of our world and attribute motives to actions. Rationalising or understanding our actions might sound like this:

- *Jonathan grabbed my biscuit because he thought it was his*
- *Stacey was unkind; she did not like my drawing, but she liked Helen's because she knew Helen would like hers*
- *I only took Sid's crayons because they draw better than mine, and he wouldn't let me use them if I asked first.*

When children are developmentally unable to use mental state talk, or feel anxious about letting themselves be known, we can provide this running commentary for them.

- *You left the room because you thought Adel might laugh at you.*
- *You thought I wanted a pen, so you gave me Jem's.*
- *You are SO proud of the work, and it looks like you are not sure how to manage the big feelings.*

As adults in the room, our job here includes not always being certain of mental states but, rather, being curious and open-minded, aware of different possibilities and, in many cases, being able to sit with 'not-knowing' (Welstead et al., 2018). Sometimes a more tentative approach is more helpful:

Sal asked you to help with the project, and I wonder if you felt unsure about what the task was. Perhaps you said something unkind to get out of helping because, right then, you could not think of a better way of getting out of it. Maybe the frustration meant you pushed Sal's model off the table. I can see you are not happy with yourself.

In therapeutic work, mental state talk, or the use of reflective language, opens up a space for curiosity (Halfon et al., 2017). Using prefaces such as:

- *I wonder if...*
- *It looks like maybe...*
- *I'm thinking you might....*

before offering a theory of what happened and the feelings around events means we are not giving a pupil a commentary based on our interpretation, as if they are accurate. CYP may correct us, deny the mental state, or shrug their shoulders. That's fine. We demonstrate interest and offer our mature thinking skills and years of experience in attempting to process what motivation, beliefs, wishes, feelings, and thoughts could be behind behaviours and actions, but we bear in mind that we cannot know and that the pupil might not be ready to know or able to tolerate the idea that you

Cognition

know. The pupil may have an awareness of their own that more closely matches their own mental state.

Teaching how our brains work can be helpful. One of the ways that cognition of brain processes may reassure us and help to rationalise feelings and thoughts is by normalising them.

Normalising

Bear and Knobe (2017) noted that children often align ideas about what is or is not normal with ideas of what is good or bad. Providing CYP information about what is 'normal' – meaning everyday, part of a predictable pattern, commonplace or unexceptional – based on facts, statistics, theory, and data, rather than judgements, can help to break this link. Thoughts and feelings are information our brains use to inform us about the internal and external world in order for us to negotiate our way through experiences. Understanding that it is common to feel a range of emotions and to think a profusion of thoughts can help us to understand that feelings and thoughts can be helpful rather than good or bad.

Normalising as a helping skill relies on the premise that if we understand the thought behind a behaviour, it makes sense of our actions and that we can then imagine or believe that many other people having that thought would act in that way. In the cognitive behaviour model of psychotherapy, the experience of distress is normalised (Dudley et al., 2007). It really is OK not to be OK. The experience of normalisation can reduce feelings of stigma and increase feelings of inclusion. Knowing and understanding that thoughts or actions are within a range of ordinary human experience can help us not to enter cycles of negative thoughts and actions or punish ourselves for our perceived shortcomings (Center for Substance Abuse Treatment (US), 2014; Dudley et al., 2007). Normalising can be a portal to acceptance, and acceptance can be a prelude to letting go; when we 'get it', we can work with it (Svinhufvud et al., 2017).

Normalising is not the panacea for everything or everyone. Normalising can have negative impacts such as:

- suggesting normal or frequently experienced feelings do not require any additional support
- implying that experiences and feelings are not painful or difficult, as they are universal
- appearing to minimise the pupil's lived experiences
- giving a message that the pupil is not exceptional or having unique experiences.

We need to hold in mind that normalising without attention and care could leave a pupil wondering why they are struggling with normality, presumably when others do not struggle in the same way (Svinhufvud et al., 2017). Not managing with 'normal' life is normal. It may be that some challenges, in some situations, at some stages in our lives cause us to struggle for some time. Not many human life responses or reactions can be generalised across all people and throughout time. Normalising means giving the message that feelings or thoughts are usual and common but not necessarily universal and certainly not easy to work through.

Theory of parts

Explaining to pupils from an early age that the brain has parts working hard on different jobs helps to explain why we often feel complex feelings or think conflicting thoughts. In layman's terms, the thinking, feeling, and survival brain parts communicate together,

34

collaboratively or conflictingly, all trying to ensure safety, comfort, and well-being. When we accept that inner conflict will be a regular experience, it can be helpful. Knowing that inner parts are all alike in their motivations, all seeking the best for us, it might help to reframe 'good and bad' as having a more realistic 'helpful, unhelpful, mis-informed, skilled or mistaken' intent. In the growing field of the psychology of parts (Noricks, 2011) and internal family systems therapy (Spiegel, 2017), parts are seen as serving roles that keep us functioning in the environments and relationships that we inhabit.

- *The part of you that so wants to belong with the group would do almost anything to be included.*
- *The part of you that likes to be kind really does not want to treat Nan like the rest of the group does.*

In play, we may often observe conflicting characters wanting different things. Spiegel (2017) described how a player can explore their interior life and motivations of different parts when they act out narratives or tell stories about characters. Play with resources can be viewed, given some distance and looked at from different perspectives, as an exploration of different outlooks or qualities of various internal parts (Halfon et al., 2017). The understanding of the therapeutic role of play includes being able to look at and manipulate experiences externally using play resources, such as toys in small world play and peers in dramatic or imaginative play. At any age, we may represent parts of ourselves as characters in stories; metaphor and symbolism help us to mentalise and develop our emotion regulation skills, as we extend our ability to sit with complex and uncertain experiences and feelings (Halfon et al., 2017):

- *The goat is butting the pig, but the pig is not moving. I wonder if the goat feels like it wants to move the pig, but the pig isn't even noticing.*
- *The goat is working hard to try and make things happen, but it's not getting anywhere.*

The play here could represent a part of the player who wants to change or move on, while another part is stuck.

While we teach pupils about parts of self in a theoretical way, generalising, giving information, and allowing pupils to decide whether the model is helpful to them or not, we allow them to make connections in their play and their experiences rather than offer our thoughts on where story and reality might converge. Teaching the theory or ideas of parts is one strategy; reflecting on play as a story or imagined world is another. In the latter, stories in play that an onlooker might feel represents parts rather than different individual characters is not explicitly or verbally communicated.

Part of you wanted the sweets, but another part of you remembered the dentist this morning and doesn't want any more fillings.

This is communicating the theory of parts to help someone understand their mixed feelings.

The big dog ignored the little dog when it wanted to play.

This is saying what you see in someone's play but does not verbalise your gut instincts that this is linked to your understanding that this person thinks they are too big to play anymore but often regrets this.

Cognition

Play and stories carry a complexity of meanings, and their role is to play out a metaphor that makes sense or a symbolic representation that provides safety. Interpretation can undo, muddle, or confuse any sense the metaphor offered and might blow apart the safety that externalising and symbolising creates. Cognition can seep in slowly, just as it may arrive like the flash of a light bulb coming on. Brain connections happen when we are ready to hear, see, or understand new information or when understanding has a place where it fits with what we already know. Like the pig and the goat, however hard the goat works, things only happen when the pig is ready to move. Play happens before our conscious thought can express or work out meaning. If we use mental state talk in play, then reflecting on the play, and not linking what is played out to the pupil's life, is the way to go.

Cognitive approaches to better mental health in school staff

A study on stress in teachers in Germany (Schwarzer et al., 2021) found similar well-being issues for teachers as reports from the Education Support (2020) and NASUWT (2019) in the UK. These were:

- symptoms of irritability
- tiredness
- anxiety
- poor sleep.

These indicators of poor mental health and their underlying stressors lead to less effective teaching, more costs from absenteeism, and significant detriment to teachers' physical, emotional, and social health. Increasing skills in mentalisation and developing knowledge and understanding of the mental states of self and of others can improve teacher mental health (Schwarzer et al., 2021). Taylor (2012) set out the responsibility we have to the school workforce and their well-being and created a model he believed would support adults working with children who have experienced trauma and disorganised attachment. The MAT (mentalising, attachment, trauma) model acknowledged that many of us work with highly vulnerable pupils, but having the ability to mentalise gives staff the ability to not get 'drawn in' or 'catch' the trauma and damaging stress from these pupils (Taylor, 2012).

Increasing understanding of psychological processes is helpful in supporting our good mental health. When we make sense of experiences, behaviours, and relationships, the cognition or mentalisation informs our attribution and belief systems. Understanding may lead both to acceptance and to adaptation. Once we understand, we feel better because knowledge can be power. Only when we can 'see' (mentalise) internal and external states and their cause and effects can we choose to change. Bateman and Fonagy (2013) reported that when we build our capacity to mentalise during stressful situations, it can increase emotional well-being and decrease the escalation of stress. People who can think about and reflect on challenges are more likely to trust others to be helpful and believe that they themselves can manage. They are also able to be creative and adaptable.

There are risks to staff well-being in cognitive approaches to improving their mental health. Some may experience challenging outcomes of increased mentalisation (Welstead et al., 2018). We may become aware of negative feelings toward pupils that we were previously not aware of. This can leave us feeling regret for missed opportunities to be helpful. Feelings of sadness or anger may increase when reflection on the pupil's life experiences create a sense of helplessness that this cannot be altered.

Theory of parts

Researchers in one study with teachers found that understanding and awareness of self, developed through training and practice of parts theory, increased ability to more fully understand the inner world of others (Böckler et al., 2017). The teachers in the study identified and named many inner parts; some parts had strong attributes, while others were more depleted. In contrast to the theory that we are more susceptible to perceiving negative judgements about ourselves (Muller-Prinzler et al., 2019), Böckler et al. (2017) reported that the research participants struggled more to identify parts in themselves we might classify as negative. Their findings were, however, that being able to acknowledge or tolerate parts that were often denied was most helpful in leading to improvements in understanding others more fully and clearly.

Psychodynamic theory suggests that we all have 'blind spots' to some of our traits and biases (Chin et al., 2012). When unable to recognise internal challenging and socially rejected emotional states, we may project our disavowed states onto others.

- *I don't really get angry. You must be the one holding the anger.*
- *I do not believe I am sad. I see sadness in you.*

It is easy to see that in this attribution to others, or outward projection, of feelings and behaviours that we are unable to accept reside in us will mean seeing others through a lens that obscures their true self in our need to obscure parts of our full person. Discovering and accepting newly recognised parts of our makeup, while challenging, can be helpful to us and change how we relate to others. Support for staff to develop new insights is essential if we are to increase teachers' mental well-being and avoid the risks that change can bring. Time for reflection within a supervisory relationship can offer such a space.

Staff supervision

Austin (2010) advocated for the role of consultancy supervision for staff in schools. A supervision space and supervisory relationship support personal development as teachers reflect and develop new insights and awareness (Anna Freud National Centre for Children and Families, n.d.; Barnado's Scotland, 2020; Hanley, 2017; Swan & Riley, 2015). Supervision is not management but, rather, a time when the normal experience of growing pains and the discomfort often associated with change are contained. Dowling and Hodson (2021) made the point that other professionals charged with supporting and protecting CYP have long had supervision to support their emotional well-being and personal and professional development.

Cognition

Supervision, sometimes called consultancy, is about giving space for staff to be curious and creative about their practice. In a safe, collaborative relationship, at best with someone external to the setting, developing insight and experiencing supportive challenge offers opportunities for exploring when we may misattribute motivations to others. We can reflect and be curious about our own behaviours and cognitions, noticing without judgement when they could be detrimental to our teaching, our relationships, and our own emotional and physical health. Austin's (2010) research demonstrated the value staff members gave to regular supervision sessions and reported how the opportunity to talk to a 'neutral', external supervisor helped them make connections to the way past experiences and relationships were impacting in their present professional, as well as personal, lives. Knowing, realising, and becoming aware of past influences on current experiences offers the opportunity to change. Without change in behaviours, awareness can still alter thoughts and feelings in ways that are beneficial to the supervisee, the pupils they work with, and the school at which they work.

Support from internal school sources, such as peers, colleagues, or line managers, will not offer the same level of freedom to speak without censor. We all edit our communications in light of how we believe we may be perceived. An external supervisor can feel like someone who plays no role in the supervisee's life other than receiving, containing, and either returning content to the supervisee in a more manageable or adaptive form, or metaphorically allowing the supervisee to leave the discarded, no longer relevant, thoughts and feelings behind after the session.

Support in the staff room is one of the things that we value and makes the job better. Support from staff can feel good and be good for us and for our professional work (Wolgast & Fischer, 2017). Support from colleagues may feel good but actually be harmful to our well-being and to our classroom practice. Support given in good faith can feel hard and distressing and, without space to process and reflect, be detrimental to us personally and professionally. Sharing challenges and vulnerability may elicit a variety of responses:

I am running out of ideas with Sam and Greg, Whatever I have tried, they just keep disrupting the class and never getting their work done.
I know, it is the same in my classes. I just tell them if they want to waste their time that is fine but let the rest of us get on please. Nothing gets through to them.

Such an exchange may lead to feelings of relief, 'It's not just me', and a sense of affirmation 'I am a good teacher. They are unteachable'. The interaction suggests the task of teaching these pupils is hopeless and that there is no way forward – end of discussion.

Different responses may lead to feelings of not being 'good enough' and that others now think we are not managing.

- *Oh? Sam and Greg? I find they can be hard to engage, but once they realise you mean what you say and will not stand for any messing, they both produce pretty good work.*
- *Sam and Greg work really well in my classes. Perhaps we could grab half an hour after class to look at what I find works well.*

Someone with no experience of the pupils in question is more able to listen to your experience without comparing it to their experience and, if in a supervisory role, can let you know you have been heard and understood, only then helping you to explore your feelings. This experience of being heard, understood. and validated can open up more space for thinking ahead and creative reflection on ways to move forward.

- *You are feeling like nothing you try is working for these two pupils. That must be difficult, and you are using a lot of energy but feeling you are getting nowhere. Right now, you don't see any chances for change.*
- *I wonder how you feel in class while this is happening?*
- *Can you think of other times you have felt like this? Maybe this situation feels familiar to you?*
- *I wonder if you have any ideas about how their behaviours serve them in the classroom. How might distracting others and not attempting their work be addressing any unmet needs for Sam or for Greg?*

Using knowledge as a springboard, we can think about environments and relationships, engaging our thinking brains to develop insights that inform practices which may alter how we feel. Having knowledge of models of human behaviours can give us a structure within which to develop hypotheses. In the illustrative example of Sam and Greg, the model of the four 'Crucial Cs' (Lew & Bettner, 1998) offers us an opportunity to reflect on unmet needs; in this case: connect, count, courage, and capable. Together, the teacher and supervisor might think about how Greg or Sam need to connect, know they count, are capable, or have courage, or they may fear that they do not count, are not capable, lack courage, and that connection leads to negative experiences rather than positive. In a supervision session, a member of school staff might use some time to think about how Greg or Sam needs to feel good, or just not feel bad, how behaviours of distracting others and not attempting the work tasks might be helping to meet psychological needs or avoid emotional harms. If some insights are reached, they could then inform next steps in classroom management to create safety for Greg and Sam or appropriate challenge for them.

Conclusion

Many theorists believe that understanding and knowledge of 'what is going on' are helpful to our mental health and to our relationships. Knowledge of self, when accompanied by compassion for self, can reduce anxiety and increase feelings of having control in our world. Knowledge and understanding of others typically create space for compassion and less need for defensiveness in responses to challenges within relationships. Mentalisation and normalisation can help us to give permission and acceptance to both ourselves and others to feel the way that we do. 'Until you make the unconscious conscious, it will direct your life and you will call it fate' is a quotation paraphrased from the work of Carl Jung (1959). Knowing and awareness of inner thoughts and processes helps us not to feel at the whim of the external world. Feeling we have agency because we are armed with understanding is good for our mental health. Having cognition and practicing self-acceptance is recognised by Carl Rogers (1995), the 'father' of person-centred counselling, as literally life changing. Self-acceptance, feeling that who and how you are is good enough, can be stress-busting. Giving opportunities for pupils to develop knowledge and understanding of themselves and their social context is key to supporting mental well-being. Everyday interactions provide opportunities for thinking about how to sustain and enhance good mental health.

Cognition

REFLECTION TASK 1: WHO AM I IN MY ROLE IN SCHOOL?

Can you list the non-teaching roles you undertake in your day-to-day work in school?

How do you have to be in those additional roles?

Which of these ways of being comes most readily for you, and which parts of your role do you most struggle with?

Do you sometimes notice you acted with a student in a way that immediately took you back to how you felt or behaved with your parent or carer?

How hard do you find it to accept praise for your work?

How often do you 'wallow' in your successes?

Would you change either of these things about you?

References

Anna Freud National Centre for Children and Families (n.d.) *Supporting Staff Wellbeing in Schools*. London: Anna Freud National Centre for Children and Families. Available from: https://www.annafreud.org/media/7026/3rdanna-freud-booklet-staff-wellbeing-final.pdf [Accessed 23rd November 2021].

American Psychological Association (APA) Dictionary of Psychology (n.d.) *Cognition*. Available from: https://dictionary.apa.org/cognition [Accessed 24th May 2021].

Austin, D. (2010) Introducing consultancy supervision in a primary school for children with social, emotional and behavioural difficulties. *Emotional and Behavioural Difficulties*, 15 (2), 125–139.

Barnado's Scotland (2020) *Supervision in Education: Healthier Schools For All: Barnardo's Scotland Report on the Use of Professional or Reflective Supervision in Education*. Illford, Essex: Barnado's.

Bateman, A. and Fonagy, P. (2013) Mentalization-based treatment. *Psychoanalytic Inquiry*, 33(6), 595–613.

Bear, A. and Knobe, J. (2017) Normality: Part descriptive, part prescriptive. *Cognition*, 167(October), 25–37.

Blackard (2012) *Say What You See for Parents and Teachers*. Austin, Texas: Language of Listening.

Blakemore, S.-J. and Frith, U. (2005) *The Learning Brain: Lessons for Education*. Oxford: Blackwell Publishing Ltd.

Böckler, A., Herrmann, L., Trautwein, F.-M., Holmes, T. and Singer, T. (2017) Know thy selves: Learning to understand oneself increases the ability to understand others. *Cognitive Enhancement*, 1, 197–209.

Borg, S. (2003) Teacher cognition in language teaching: A review of research on what language teachers think, know, believe, and do. *Language Teaching*. Cambridge University Press, 36 (2), 81–109. Available from: doi: 10.1017/S0261444803001903

Center for Substance Abuse Treatment (US). (2014) *Trauma-Informed Care in Behavioral Health Services*. Substance Abuse and Mental Health Services Administration (US). Available from: https://pubmed.ncbi.nlm.nih.gov/24901203/

Chin, J., Mrazek, M. and Schooler, J. (2012) Blind spots to the self: Limits in knowledge of mental contents and personal predispositions. In: Vazire, S. and Wilson, T. (eds.) *Handbook of Self-knowledge*. New York: The Guilford Press. 77–89.

Department for Education (DfE) (2019) *Early Career Framework*. London: DfE. Available from: https://www.gov.uk/government/publications/early-career-framework [Accessed 15th July 2021].

Dowling, M. and Hodson, M. (2021) The need for health and well-being. In: Maisey, D. and Campbell-Barr, V. (eds.) *Why do Teachers Need to Know About Child Development?* London: Bloomsbury. 25–42.

Dreikurs, R., Grunwald, B. and Pepper, F. (1971) *Maintaining Sanity in the Classroom: Illustrated Teaching Techniques*. New York: Harper & Row.

Dudley, R., Bryant, C., Hammond, K., Siddle, R., Kingdon, D. and Turkington, D. (2007) Techniques in cognitive behavioural therapy: Using normalising in Schizophrenia. *Journal of the Norwegian Psychological Association (Tidsskrift for Kognitiv Terapi)* 44, 562–571.

Education Support (2020) Teacher wellbeing index. Available from: https://www.educationsupport .org.uk/resources/research-reports/teacher-wellbeing-index-2020 [Accessed 23rd November 2021].

Fonagy, P. (2008) The mentalization-focused approach to social development. In: Busch, F. (ed.) *Mentalization: Theoretical Considerations, Research Findings, and Clinical Implications*. New York: The Analytic Press. 3–56.

Fonagy, P. and Allison, E. (2012) What is mentalization? The concept and its foundations in developmental research. In Midgley, N. and Vrouva, I. (eds.) *Minding the Child: Mentalization-based Interventions with Children, Young People and Their Families*. Hove, East Sussex: Routledge. 11–34.

Frith, C. and Frith, U. (2006) The neural basis of mentalizing. *Neuron* 50 (4) 531–534.

Gerhardt, S. (2004) *Why Love Matters: How Affection Shapes a Baby's Brain*. Hove: Brunner-Routledge.

Halfon, S., Bekar, O. and ra Gürleyen, B. (2017) An empirical analysis of mental state talk and affect regulation in two single-cases of psychodynamic child therapy. *Psychotherapy*, 54 (2), 207–219.

Hanley, T. (2017) Supporting the emotional labour associated with teaching: Considering a pluralistic approach to group supervision. *Pastoral Care in Education*, 35 (4), 253–266.

Horowitz, M. (1998) *Cognitive Psychodynamics: From Conflict to Character*. New York: John Wiley & Sons Inc.

Howe, D. (2011) *Attachment Across the Life Course: A Brief Introduction*. Basingstoke: Palgrave Macmillan.

Husbands, C. and Pearce, J. (2012) *What Makes Great Pedagogy? Nine Claims from Research*. Nottingham: NCTL.

Jung, C. (1959) *Aion*. New York: Routledge.

Kerns, K., Mathews, B., Koehn, A., Williams, C. and Siener-Ciesla, S. (2015) Assessing both safe haven and secure base support in parent–child relationships. *Attachment & Human Development*, 17 (4), 337–353. Available from: doi: 10.1080/14616734.2015.1042487

Kesner, J. (2000) Teacher characteristics and the quality of child–teacher relationships. *Journal of School Psychology*, 28 (2), 133–149.

Kourkoutasa, E. and Giovazolias, T. (2015) School-based counselling work with teachers: An integrative model. *The European Journal of Counselling Psychology*, 3 (2), 137–158.

Lew, A. (2002) Helping Children cope in an increasingly threatening World: Four cornerstones of emotional well-being. *The Family Journal: Counseling and Therapy for Couples and Families*, April, 10 (2), 134–138.

Lew, A. and Bettner, B. (1998) *Responsibility in the Classroom: A Teacher's Guide to Understanding and Motivating Students (Raising Kids Who Can Series)*. Newton Centre: Connexions Press.

Maisey, D. and Campbell-Barr, V. (eds.) (2021) *Why do Teachers Need to Know About Child Development? Strengthening Professional Identity and Well-Being*. London: Bloomsbury.

Marvin, R., Cooper, G., Hoffman, K. and Powell, B. (2002) The circle of security project: Attachment-based intervention with caregiver–pre-school child dyads. *Attachment & Human Development*, 4 (1), 107–124.

McRory, E. (2021) Transformation seminar: Childhood Trauma and the Brain: What have we learnt from neuroscience? March 10. Available from: https://www.youtube.com/watch?v=uj-8D7L-coE

Monsen, J., Woolfson, L. and Boyle, J. (eds.) (2021) *Why Do Teachers Need to Know About Psychology? Strengthening Professional Identity and Well-Being.* London: Bloomsbury.

Müller-Pinzler, L., Czekalla, N., Mayer, A., Stoltz, D., Gazzola, V., Keysers, C. Paulus, F. and Krach, S. (2019) Negativity-bias in forming beliefs about own abilities. *Scientific Reports*, 9, 14416. Available from: doi.org/10.1038/s41598-019-50821-w.

NASUWT (2019) Teachers' mental health in the UK: Evidence from the NASUWT's big question survey 2019. Available from: https://www.nasuwt.org.uk/uploads/assets/uploaded/30c31a30-b070-44f1-8e9f009b650bb350.pdf [Accessed 04th August 2021].

Nelson, R., Spence-Thomas, K. and Taylor, C. (2015) *What Makes Great Pedagogy and Great Professional Development: Final Report: Teaching Schools R&D Network National Themes Project 2012–14.* Nottingham: NCTL.

Noricks, J. (2011) *Parts Psychology: A Trauma-Based, Self-State Therapy for Emotional Healing.* Los Angeles: New University Press.

Ofsted (2019) Education inspection framework: Overview of research. Ref. 180045. Available from: https://www.gov.uk/government/publications/education-inspection-framework-overview-of-research [Accessed 04th August 2021].

Perry, T., Lea, R., Jørgensen, C.R., Cordingley, P., Shapiro, K. and Youdell, D. (2021) *Cognitive Science in the Classroom.* London: Education Endowment Foundation (EEF). Available from: https://educationendowmentfoundation.org.uk/evidence-summaries/evidence-reviews/cognitive-science-approaches-in-the-classroom/ [Accessed 15th July 2021].

Riley, P. (2010) *Attachment Theory and the Teacher-Student Relationship.* Oxford: Routledge.

Rogers, C. (1995) What understanding and acceptance mean to me. *Journal of Humanistic Psychology*, 35 (4), 7–22.

Saxner, R. (2021) The crucial Cs in practice. *The Journal of Individual Psychology*, 77 (2), 145–153.

Schwarzer, N., Nolte, T., Fonagy, P., Griem, J., Kieschke, U. and Gingelmaier, S. (2021) The relationship between global distress, mentalizing and well-being in a German teacher sample. *Curr Psychology*, Published online 26 February. Available from: doi: 10.1007/s12144-021-01467-3

Spiegel, L. (2017) *Internal Family Systems Therapy with Children.* New York: Routledge.

Svinhufvud, K., Voutilainen, L. and Weiste, E. (2017) Normalizing in student counseling: Counselors' responses to students' problem descriptions. *Discourse Studies*, 19 (2), 196–215.

Swan, P. and Riley, P. (2015) Social connection: Empathy and mentalization for teachers. *Pastoral Care in Education*, 33 (4), 220–233.

Taylor, C. (2012) *Empathic Care for Children with Disorganized Attachments: A Model for Mentalizing, Attachment and Trauma-informed Care.* London: Jessica Kingsley Publishers.

The Children's Society (2021) The good childhood report 2021. Available from: https://www.childrenssociety.org.uk/information/professionals/resources/good-childhood-report-2021. [Accessed 23rd January 2022].

Tompkins, V., Benigno, J., Kiger Lee, B. and Wright, B. (2018) The relation between parents' mental state talk and children's social understanding: A meta-analysis. *Social Development*, 27 (2), 223–246.

UK Trauma Council (2020) The guidebook to childhood trauma and the brain. Available from: https://uktraumacouncil.link/documents/CHILDHOOD-TRAUMA-AND-THE-BRAIN-SinglePages.pdf [Accessed 09th January 2022].

Verschueren, K. and Koomen, H. (2012) Teacher–child relationships from an attachment perspective. *Attachment & Human Development*, 14 (3), 205–211.

Vollmann, M., Sprang, S. and van den Brink F. (2019) Adult attachment and relationship satisfaction: The mediating role of gratitude toward the partner. *Journal of Social and Personal Relationships*. 36 (11–12), 3875–3886.

Wascher, C., Kulachi, I. Langley, E. and Shaw R. (2018) How does cognition shape social relationships? *Philosophical Transactions of the Royal Society, B*, 373 (1756). doi: 10.1098/rstb.2017.0293

Welstead, H., Patrick, J, Russ, C. Cooney, G. Mulvenna, C. Maclean, C. and Polnay, A. (2018) Mentalising skills in generic mental healthcare settings: Can we make our day-to-day interactions more therapeutic? *BJPsych Bulletin*, 42, 102–108.

Wolgast, A. and Fischer, N. (2017) You are not alone: Colleague support and goal-oriented cooperation as resources to reduce teachers' stress. *Social Psychology of Education*, 20, 97–114.

Wu, J., Liu, M. and Lin, W. (2021) Impact of Teacher's mental state talk on young Children's theory of mind: A quasi-experiment study. *Frontiers in Psychology*, 26 March. Available from: doi: 10.3389/fpsyg.2021.668883.

Zull, J. (2002) *The Art of Changing the Brain: Enriching the Practice of Teaching by Exploring the Biology of Learning*. Sterling: Stylus Publishing.

Chapter 3

Compassion

What is compassion?

Compassion is the awareness of distress in self or others and the feeling of care, the desire to help to make things better, and the effort to bring about relief and improvement (Gilbert et al., 2017; Miralles et al., 2019). Compassion is a powerful connection between people; accepting that we all experience the need for compassion at some point, that pain is part of life, includes not only the times we give support but also the times we need to be able to accept support from others (Esch & Stefano, 2011; Strauss et al., 2016).

Compassion may be experienced as:

- a feeling
- an action
- the emotion and intention behind an action
- a way of being (Porges, 2017).

The emotional skills used in helping professions could be summed up as 'compassion'. Compassionate helpers may demonstrate personal skills such as:

- being warm, genuine, accepting, non-judgemental and trustworthy
- wanting to help others, while not needing to meet their own needs by helping others – not needing to rescue, not needing to feel good through solving others' problems by directing them to a solution
- having a genuine interest in others and in their story, experiences, and feelings
- celebrating the uniqueness of each person and having an open curiosity about how it is to live in their world.

Being able to contain and not be overwhelmed by the distress of others is also important in a compassionate response – when you feel for the person rather than share in their emotion (Dowling, 2018; Strauss et al., 2016). Compassionate care means maintaining perspective and not being activated by, or joining with, the suffering

DOI: 10.4324/9781003277903-4

of the other. Compassion suggests that, while feeling for the other, keeping some emotional distance enables the compassionate helper to be helpful. Staying 'apart', caring while not becoming entangled in the pain or grief, means being able to think and act with more clarity and efficacy. Our ability to notice and care when another is struggling and have the desire to help, when accompanied by an ability to not become overwhelmed or damaged by the enormity of situations, takes skill and wisdom (Chapman, 2019; Gilbert et al., 2017).

We may be used to the notion of having compassion for others but have not reflected as much on the idea of having compassion toward ourselves. We may notice that some people appear to be 'compulsive care-givers' – compassionate toward others while neglecting to offer such sensitivity and care toward themselves. Some of us actively seek out opportunities to be compassionate toward others but seem unable to seek or accept compassion for ourselves. Giving and receiving compassion are not always in balance. Awareness of the 'flow' between compassion for others, for ourselves, and from others can lead to a healthier balance in our social relationships and sustain our internal reservoirs of energy and optimism (Hermanto & Zuroff, 2016).

Compassion is an attitude toward ourselves or others that is about understanding and care. This is not the understanding we thought about in the chapter on cognition. Compassion may be informed by cognitive knowledge and understanding, that is a 'top-down' process, from the knowing brain to the feeling brain (Gilbert, 2021). It may be more likely to be prompted through a 'bottom-up' process, in which information from the feeling brain which developed from the experience of an emotional response to a person or situation feeds up to the thinking brain. Compassion is informed by innate understanding of what it is to be human and of our inborn ability to be attuned to others, which may be blended with learned knowledge. Marc Bekoff (2000), an expert in animal behaviour, recognised that many animals are able to feel compassion, amongst other emotions. Compassion and empathy appear to be innate in us and in other animals who do not need to know any theory about why others feel the way that they do in order for them to care.

Internal family systems (IFS) therapy, a model of therapy based on the theory of parts, talks about a core 'self' in each of us that is innately compassionate (Schwartz, 2021; Schwartz & Sweezy, 2019). IFS practitioners believe that we all have a core essential self that is wise, compassionate, curious, and creative. As we experience the challenges of life, we develop parts that help us to navigate the world. In terms of IFS therapy, we develop protective parts to shield us from emotional pain (Anderson, 2021; Schwartz, 2021; Spiegel, 2017). Parts of us 'manage' how we interact with the world in order that we 'get by', 'fit in', and cope. Other parts 'firefight' when an escalation is needed to avoid harm to our inner self. In Schwartz's (1997) model, the self is innately compassionate and is a calm centre, while managers and firefighters are developed to protect us when we experience dangerous or damaging life events or times when we felt socially or emotionally vulnerable.

Reading about compassion from authors and researchers across a breadth of disciplines illustrates that compassion is seen as relevant to philosophy, biology, religion, psychology, psychotherapy, culture, politics, and other areas of personal and social worlds. Understanding more about the role of compassion may help us to better realise its nature. Whether we learn compassion, have innate compassion, or there is a blend of an inborn capability for compassion that is nurtured by experience is of interest because compassion is a powerful force for connection, social justice, and cohesion.

Some suggestions from research into the evolutionary development of compassion are that compassion evolved:

- as part of the motivation to care for the needs of vulnerable offspring
- as a response to preferences in mate selection
- as a medium for building and bonding wider social group relationships (Gilbert, 2021; Goetz et al., 2010; Miralles et al., 2019).

Compassion may be a preferred trait in partnerships, it may increase the likelihood of survival of children, and it may cement group and community relationships and a sense of tribe or belonging.

Researchers with an interest in neurobiology have explored how our genetics or our physiology influence our ability to experience compassion. Genetic tendencies and hormonal influences, as well as differences in expression and acceptance of compassion, may be amplified or selected by environmental contexts or cultural norms and expectations (Esch & Stefano, 2011; Gilbert, 2021; Taylor et al., 2000). Polyvagal theory (Porges, 2011) recognised early evolutionary nerve structures that governed the fight, flight, and freeze responses to threat, with later developed associated structures to support social engagement. Our ability to offer compassion is impacted by our physiological state (Gerbarg et al., 2019). When we feel safe and cared for, we are not in a state of fight or flight, and we are more able to experience feelings of compassion for others. Porges (2017) explained ways, such as breathing exercises and meditation, that we can calm our arousal to threat, increase our feelings of safety, and therefore, gain capacity for compassion. When our need and our capacity for social engagement come online, we are able to feel compassion, further building connection to others.

Taylor et al. (2000) noted that the research and literature on the threat response of fight or flight has over-shadowed another response to stress: that of 'tend and befriend'. Widely understood as a basic survival response to threat, fight, flight, or freeze are ways an individual best ensures their survival in threatening situations. Tend and befriend may be an effective prosocial response in small groups facing threat. Seeking and giving social support and looking after and showing friendship to the people you find yourself with becomes important when a challenge arises (Šolcová et al., 2022). Increasing the likelihood of survival or success may be an evolutionary function of compassion. Compassion and kindness benefit us in everyday life by building relationships within affiliated groups.

The extension of compassion as a survival strategy might be expected to be limited to those we see as our tribe (Ballatt et al., 2020). Individuals and groups may extend compassion most readily to those we feel are 'like us' or those who could be of benefit to us. The debate over the nature of compassion includes a consideration of why we may offer compassion when it involves risk and cost to our own well-being (Gilbert, 2021; Goetz et al., 2010; Strauss et al., 2016). To offer compassion with no apparent benefit to ourselves suggests a possible motivation from a belief in 'doing the right thing'. Williams (2008) suggested that the nature of compassion is to be outward-looking and, as a personal moral imperative, is linked to our sense of social justice and to our sense of ourselves. The context of our lives and the ethos of our societies may have impacted humanity's ability to feel or freely offer compassion to everyone (Williams, 2008).

Offering compassion can be linked to a conscious or unconscious evaluation of the merit of the person in need (Maestri & Monforte, 2020). Notions of innocence and perceptions of whether suffering has been in some way self-inflicted can form part of an evaluation about who deserves our compassion (Nussbaum, 1996; Williams, 2008). Baguley et al. (2020) reported that seeing someone as a fellow person, having a sense of the commonality of being human, are important for maintaining a compassionate stance. Fears of compassion fatigue, or of the limits of our ability to offer compassion, could mean that we have a sense that compassion must be judicially spent, therefore, we evaluate to whom we offer or deny our compassion (Stone, 2020).

Beliefs that feeling or offering compassion leads to fatigue or burnout are widespread (for example see Smullens, 2012; Thapa et al., 2021). Many (for example see Dowling, 2018; Esch & Stefano, 2011; Preckel et al., 2018) support a more optimistic view on compassion: that it is not solely depleting, but also enriching to the giver, and that our reservoir is refreshed, rather than used up. Compassion may lead to fatigue, or it can result in feelings of satisfaction, particularly if we feel we have been helpful. Feeling that our help has not resulted in benefits or improvements appears to lead to the likelihood of burnout (Smullens, 2012). Underlying levels of resilience and of feeling supported in the workplace increase the chance of experiencing compassion satisfaction (Bhutani et al., 2012; Thapa et al., 2021).

Joan Halifax (2012) saw kindness in balance with composure and poise as elements of compassion. Giving compassion of this nature means not giving unsustainably of ourselves. While showing kindness through tender concern, staying grounded and aware of the otherness of giver from receiver keeps the relationship safe for both. Emotional caring, with cognitive understanding, awareness, and acceptance of what is possible, what is desirable, and what serves others without disserving self, may be why compassion is sustainable and mutually beneficial.

Be kind: the kindness of compassion

Some describe kindness as a component of compassion (Neff, 2003), while others see compassion as a component of kindness (Peplak & Malti, 2021). Kindness may be employed with wisdom and thought (Ballatt et al., 2020), and it can be targeted at need with an idea of having an appropriate and helpful impact. NHS England is committed to compassion in their services, recognising that, in order to provide compassionate care, 'carers and relatives must be treated with sensitivity and kindness' (Department of Health and Social Care, 2021a). In order to ensure that compassion is at the heart of everything they do, any care they provide must include responding 'with humanity and kindness to each person's pain, distress, anxiety or need' (Department of Health and Social Care, 2021b). Calls to offer compassion could link to a recent movement asking that we all 'Be Kind'. In 2021, the BBC 'All in the Mind' programme, in association with Robin Banerjee (Green, 2021), undertook a study on kindness. In a research review on kindness, Banerjee (Hammond, 2021) discovered that acting with kindness is contagious, makes us feel less anxious, and has a feel-good factor for the protagonist.

In 2020, the Mental Health Foundation took kindness as the focus of Mental Health Week, noting that it is a courageous act to be kind. 'Have Courage' is one of The Samaritans' five tips for listening (Colombus, 2021). The Samaritans also recognise that compassion is vital to helpful listening and believe that being compassionate is not only helpful to others but also supports well-being and health for those acting with compassion (Colombus, 2021). Courage is one of the four 'Crucial C's'; it is a positive experience to see yourself as brave (Lew, 2002). Brené Brown (n.d.) talked of the need for courage in her 'Dare to Lead' initiative. Courage, for Brown, means being brave enough to be vulnerable as well as being able to have compassion for yourself.

Following the death of Felix Alexander in 2017, and Caroline Flack in 2020 (Alexander, 2021), 'Be Kind' was seen on posters and T-shirts and heard across news media and social media outlets. Acts of kindness can benefit both giver and receiver. Otake et al. (2006) acknowledged a complex link between kindness and happiness. Happy people are more likely to be kind, and kind people are more likely to be happy. Being kind can make happy people happier (Otake et al., 2006). This looks like a virtuous cycle or a tangled relationship in which it is complex to isolate cause from effect.

An acronym of 'Be Kind' offers a recipe for being kind and showing compassion:

Belief: *Believe in the child and their ability to cope, solve their own problem and heal their emotional wounds.*
Engage: *Engage with the child using your thoughts and feelings, and let them know you hear their words, you care and your intention is to truly understand.*
Knowledge: *Know yourself and recognise your own challenges, strengths and emotional triggers.*
Intention: *Have the intention to be open and to respond with compassion.*
Now: *Stay in the here and now in order to give full attention.*
Delight: *Delight in connection and in the courage of the child to speak and in your courage to truly listen.*

(Better Play, 2021)

Why does compassion matter for teachers' practice?

Attuned, sensitive, and responsive adults provide compassionate relationships for children, within which the levels of the stress hormone cortisol are regulated and return to lower levels more quickly at times of anxiety, fear, or challenge, reducing damaging immediate and long-term effects (Gerhardt, 2004; National Scientific Council on the Developing Child, 2005; Shonkoff & Phillips, 2000; Sunderland, 2016).

An adult's presence can be a balm or a blight. We can change the emotional state in others, create environments where children feel safe enough to learn, foster a caring and sharing ethos in groups, or do none of the above. Compassion is a calm, balanced, and caring stance toward others that does not seek to gain compliance or gratitude or abuse a position of power or authority. Compassion matters because there is some evidence that the gains for recipients (pupils in this case) are not inappropriately or disproportionately costly for the provider (teacher). If compassionate teachers can lower levels of cortisol in pupils in their classrooms, knowing that this has physical benefits and facilitates learning, then we want compassionate teachers in all of our schools.

Compassion

What does compassion look like in teachers' practice?

Compassionate people have several helpful ways of relating to others. Many of them are about being truly present in the moment of relating.

Being with

We often forget that 'just being there' matters more than anything. Being with is a powerful experience. Have you ever just wanted someone beside you, not for what they might say or for what they could do, but just to feel that they are there? For some of us, or with some people or at some times, being comfortable 'being' and not 'doing' is challenging. Maybe especially when you are at work and feel contracted to do, do, do. If you are busy doing, it can be hard to give your full attention to the other person or to completely stay in the moment. So much of our work role can be about changing things rather than staying with.

Compassion offers a calm space of being with, when that is what is needed to help pupils feel better. Feeling better means learning better.

Giving full attention

Giving full attention is a skill that sounds obvious and much easier than it actually often is. When an opportunity arises, if we monitor our focus on a speaker and note when we realise that we are thinking about something else, we realise how often our minds naturally drift. Thoughts can drift to things as random as whether I put apples on the shopping list or whether the grass will be dry enough to cut. The intrusive thoughts might be connected to the narrative of your speaker: this sounds just like something that happened to me, or I am not enjoying the story I am hearing. We may notice when the random wanderings of our minds mean we are not giving attention to the things we are hearing, but shifting from listening to the story we are hearing into thinking about a linked memory or feeling about ourselves also means we are not giving full attention to the speaker.

Compassion is an outward-looking stance. Compassion means turning towards the other and, through focused attention to the other, finding out what is needed to help them feel better. It might be that having attention and feeling heard was all that was needed. Having a need met creates space for moving on with other tasks.

Staying in the here and now

This is a relational skill that naturally precedes the skills for planning or acting for the future. Without truly listening and fully being with, it is likely that our actions or plans to address what we heard will not be informed by the full story. We may have started planning for 'what's next' from the beginning of the story, thus, missing important clues or subtleties that only giving full attention and being in the moment can provide.

Compassion is about the here and now. Being in the moment could be overwhelming if we are not able to be aware and wise in our practice of compassion and kindness. When we maintain balance and equanimity, all we have to do is stay with the moment, offer strength in that time, and not think about whether we can maintain this over time. Compassion accepts how it is 'just now' and works on what can be done in the present.

50

Creating a sense of safety

Feeling safe increases our ability to engage in the world. When we feel safe in relationships, we take emotional risks, deepen our connections, and can try out being whoever we want or need to be. When we are feeling safe in our environment, our fight and flight system can take a back seat, and our seeking and engagement system takes over and can discover and learn and expand our horizons. Both safe relationships and safe environments in early life are springboards to a healthy and fulfilled future. Feeling safe is not an experience universal to everyone in any environment or relationship. The level of predictability and control in a given situation is felt differently by us all, dependent on our previous experiences, personality traits, and state of emotional and physical health at the given time.

Compassion involves attunement and sensitivity to those in need and seeks ways to help to alleviate feelings of insecurity or anxiety. Compassion also involves trust in the other to manage and belief in the ability of the other to arrive at solutions that are right for them. Compassion is not about feelings of desire to control and rescue pupils by removing all risk and challenge. Compassion means sensitivity to when others have reached the edge of their ability to tolerate what is happening or how they are feeling and then seeking ways to support the other to regain their sense of feeling 'safe enough'.

Curiosity

Demonstrating interest is one of the most powerful tools for building relationships. Really listening, wanting to completely understand what is being shared, means that we are curious about what it means for the other. It means wondering whether there is anything we can helpfully offer to move the other toward feeling safer, more comfortable, and more emotionally well. Curiosity is extended to ourselves during interactions: how am I feeling as I hear this? Why might I be feeling like this? How can I help myself right now in order to focus on the other? Defensiveness is the enemy of curiosity. Curiosity emerges when we move out from our defences, which can entail bravery and courage but leads to personal growth and, often, to an experience of wonder and awe.

Being genuinely interested is part of a compassionate response to another. Compassion involves curiosity about what we need as well as about the needs of others.

Self-awareness

This relational skill is a necessary ability in order to ensure that we are fully available to others and not, without us noticing, listening through a filter that makes everything we hear fit with our own beliefs, feelings, experiences, and understanding. We offer authentic acceptance and non-judgement to others when we have reflected on the level to which we can offer them to ourselves. Self-awareness is necessary if we are to know whether compassionate responses are true compassion rather than meeting our own needs to protect and nurture those younger or more vulnerable than ourselves. Insight into our own processes helps us to see when we may be meeting our need to be the hero of the moment or to create indebtedness in others in order for us to feel good about ourselves.

People who can be compassionate toward themselves have the courage to notice when their needs are impacting on interactions. Awareness and acceptance of self increases the likelihood of insightful attunement to others.

Compassion

Staying power

Marie Delaney's (2009) book *Teaching the Unteachable* offered accessible and practical information and ideas for the classroom. The chapter 'Well I tried all those strategies and they're still unteachable' echoes the experience of so many of us in education who have struggled with challenging classes and pupils. It may also chime with us regarding all the strategies we have tried in order to change ourselves, only to find we still eat, talk, complain, or prevaricate too much, or don't maintain new plans to exercise, sleep, or socialise more.

To resist and not follow through on change is part of the human condition. The development of resistance to change begins early in childhood and becomes wired into our brains (Forsell & Åström, 2012). Change is hard for many of us, and our levels of comfort with, or resistance to, change may depend on whether we had consistent or chaotic experiences in our early lives. Consistent but negative (critical, punitive) parenting can make us fear change, as can chaotic and negative (neglectful, fearful) experiences. These parenting styles are also likely to develop insecure attachment relationships between carer and child. Consistent and kind parenting, in which more secure attachments are built, can help children to see change, like they see the world, as non-threatening and full of possibilities.

For our pupils who are anxious, fearful, resistant, or feel the need to be in control, change will take time. It challenges our ability to persevere when we try a strategy to improve the life of the classroom or an individual pupil, and it feels as though it is not working. Our resolve can be tested, as feelings of disappointment, disillusionment, and plain fatigue are experienced.

Whether we change strategies through lack of belief in their efficacy or because we feel external pressure for results, it does not allow for the time needed to continue with strategies not showing immediate results. Change takes time. Considering that the brain took time to build the current neural networks, it is understandable that time will be needed for re-wiring. Children who experienced resistance to change as a protective and safe way to be are not going to abandon tried and tested strategies of their own in a hurry. Children who do not trust others or believe what others say or those who are waiting for our compassion to slip, believing that our 'true' punishing and critical nature will be revealed, will need time to see that we do as we say and that we do care, are kind, and will travel the hard path beside them.

Compassion does not have deadlines or timeframe expectations. Compassion can extend itself when it is not destructive to the well-being of the person who gives it. If compassionate teachers are comfortable and at ease with the process, knowing they are doing what they judge to be in the best interest of another, slow but sure works and can effect lasting change for a pupil in a way that changing approaches just will not.

Compassion as a route to better mental health for teachers

Giving and receiving compassion may offer protection to teachers against the depletion from the emotional labour of the job, and from the stressful role of witness to students' experiences (Preckel et al., 2018). Neff and Seppala (2017) acknowledged that there is a developing wealth of research in support of the notion that compassion for others, but more particularly compassion for self, are beneficial to our well-being. The rewarding sense of caring for others and the meeting of our human need to connect, which is essential to a compassionate response, feed us at the times when we empathise with the pain and suffering of another (Gonzalez-Mendez & Díaz, 2021). This may potentially immunise us to the most exhausting effects of emotionally supporting our pupils. Self-compassion may play a role as a 'buffer' (Preckel et al., 2018; Gerber & Anaki, 2021) for psychological stress in the caring professions. It appears that self-compassion, or warmth towards self, can buffer the effects of stress, threat, and overwhelm (Lau et al., 2020).

Empathy is about feeling how the other feels. The word empathy is often used as a way to describe when one person can really feel what they see the other experiencing and can put themselves in the place of the other. Empathy, when experienced often, can lead to depletion and stress for the helping professional (Wilkinson et al., 2017; Williams et al., 2017). Hofmyer et al. (2020) discussed the need for a definition of compassion if we are to understand its nature and impact. They described empathic distress fatigue as being a more helpful description than compassion fatigue. This suggests that, unlike compassion, empathy may cause distress, or it does not give the empathic helper the same positive feedback given to the compassionate helper. A negative cycle of self-preservation can develop when our emotional resources are drained, leaving us unable to be empathic or sensitive in our responses to suffering in others.

The evidence that compassion does not lead to fatigue (Dowling, 2018, Hofmyer et al., 2020; Nilsson, 2014) is not universally accepted; other research identifies concerns of compassion fatigue (Cocker & Joss, 2016) and of the need for strategies to maintain compassion (Baguley et al., 2020). These differences suggest we need an agreed definition of compassion that can be more readily researched and debated. The possibility that compassion may not be as emotionally impactful on the helper as empathy might be and that it may have positive benefits for them is of interest to the helping professions. Those working in caring roles have often seen empathy as core to their work. Protecting workers from burnout is important to employers and to the experience of clients. The positive feelings created by acts of compassion have been linked to oxytocin (Dowling, 2018), a bonding hormone linked to attachment building. Oxytocin is associated with feelings of calm and connection (Moberg, 2003). Burnout and some of the negative impacts attributed to feelings of empathy for others contrasts with the buffering and even boosting effects of feelings of compassion reported in some of the literature. Rather than running out of empathy and spiralling into hopelessness or negativity, refuelling through compassion may increase energy and the ability to give and be helpful, meaning it is possible that compassion is a sustainable resource (Esch & Stefano, 2011; Mascaro et al., 2020).

Compassion as a route to better mental health for pupils

Teachers' warmth and kindness in their workplace relationships may facilitate the development of compassion in their pupils (Colaianne et al., 2020; Hilppö et al., 2019). By setting the classroom climate and ethos, we may create a feeling of calm waters or of stormy seas. Teachers' kindness also contributes to a productive learning environment. Eccles and Roeser (2016) noted that meeting the needs of pupils in adolescence, through kindness and warmth, may be most powerful for supporting their mental well-being at this stage. In adolescence, our pupils revisit the early years' developmental challenges of developing identity and of needing to feel a sense of security and belonging.

In secondary schools, the consistency of environments and relationships is very different to that of primary settings. We have more expectations of the ease and comfort of secondary age pupils with autonomy and self-direction in the school setting. We could be in danger of neglecting their ongoing need for connection to us. We know peer relationships are important to our pupils at this stage and possibly do not recognise the continuing importance of their relationship to us. Teachers see several different groups each day and have so many curriculum tasks to complete that space for connecting with pupils and building relationships is constrained. Teenagers are taking bigger psychological and cognitive risks, and we are asking them to show courage and maturity. A safe base to explore from and retreat to is just as important in adolescence as it is in toddlerhood. Compassion from teachers during adolescence may lead to better engagement, higher achievements, and better mental health (Eccles & Roeser, 2016).

The Scottish curriculum initiative, 'The Compassionate and Connected Classroom and Community' (Education Scotland, n.d. p. 5), offers a programme of instruction around knowledge and understanding of adversity and trauma. This includes the strand: 'Support children to develop compassion, empathy and tolerance in their relationships with others.'

Teachers who do not believe in their pupils' abilities to respond with compassion, tolerate strong feelings in their peers, or be part of a helpful solution, can stifle emerging compassion in pupils by not allowing for skills to develop (Hilppö et al., 2019). This may lead to a classroom where the adult is expected to demonstrate compassion, while there is no such expectation from pupils, or there is even a denial of opportunities for peers to practice compassionate acts. Compassion is an emotion which needs exercising (Peplak & Malti, 2021). A misguided desire to protect or shield children may arrest their development of compassion. Not believing in pupils' resilience denies them their right to have courage and of the personal growth gained by learning their capacity for struggle and tolerance of discomfort and distress (Chapman, 2019; Porges, 2017). Resilience has a strong correlation with good mental health; getting through hard times, knowing feelings change, and believing in your own strength build resilience. Giving messages such as 'you cannot cope' and 'this is so bad you can never come back from this' so 'you need me to save or protect you' denies the pupil the opportunity to find, nurture, and believe in their own resilience. Compassion is having the sensitivity to allow others to feel their own pain and not needing to create a world of good times and pleasure for them. This is balanced by the compassionate wisdom needed to understand when it is time, as the adult, to titrate and contain the unmanageable for the child or young person.

Conclusion

Compassion for the child in times of suffering is a natural human response. Compassion for ourselves as we struggle to be with another's pain is just as essential. Recognising our strengths and struggles is part of being kind to ourselves. The exact multi-facets of compassion may not yet be established or clear-cut, but caring and wanting to help are agreed upon as essential elements of compassion. The increasing evidential support for the benefits of offering compassion over offering empathy is based on the belief that compassion may not be as exhausting of our reserves and that, in fact, the element of being motivated to help can help to regulate our own emotions (Gilbert, 2021; Singer & Engert, 2019; Weng et al., 2013). Knowing that observing and being around others demonstrating compassion, kindness, and warmth is contagious and leads to feelings of well-being, helps to establish the role of compassion in the classroom as a benefit for all.

REFLECTION TASK 2: COMPASSION

How do you perceive *yourself* in terms of personal strengths and challenges in supporting friends and family? I am …

What do you know or think *others* say about your personal strengths and challenges in supporting them? You are …

List the skills that you feel you naturally employ to build relationships and support pupils' well-being in your work role.

What do you know or think others say about your personal strengths and challenges in supporting people in your work role?

How much time and energy do you spend on caring for others?

How much time and energy do you spend on caring for yourself?

Would you like to change the balance of where you direct your time, energy and care?

References

Alexander, E. (2021) A year on from Caroline Flack's suicide, we have learnt nothing about being kind: Kindness requires work and emotional intelligence; we need to practise it more. *In Harper's Bazar.* Available from: https://www.harpersbazaar.com/uk/culture/a35508909/caroline-flack-be-kind-comment/ [Accessed 13th December 2021].

Anderson, F. (2021) *Transcending Trauma: Healing Complex PTSD with Internal Family Systems.* Eau Claire, WI: PESI Publishing, Inc.

Baguley, S., Dev, V., Fernando, A. and Consedine, N. (2020) How do health professionals maintain compassion over time? Insights from a study of compassion in health. *Frontiers in Psychology,* 29 December, 11. Available from: doi:10.3389/fpsyg.2020.564554

Ballatt, J., Campling, P. and Maloney, C. (2020) *Intelligent Kindness: Rehabilitating the Welfare State.* 2nd ed. Cambridge: Cambridge University Press.

Bekoff, M. (2000) Animal emotions: Exploring passionate natures. *BioScience,* October, 50 (10), 861–870.

Better Play (2021) *Be Kind.* Available from: http://www.better-play.co.uk/wp/?page_id=381 [Accessed 12th January 2022].

Bhutani, J., Bhutani, S., Balhara, Y. and Kalra, S. (2012) Compassion fatigue and burnout amongst clinicians: A medical exploratory study. *Indian Journal of Psychological Medicine,* 34 (4), 332–337. Available at: doi: 10.4103/0253-7176.108206

Brown, B. (n.d.) Dare to lead hub. Available from: https://daretolead.brenebrown.com/ [Accessed 26th December 2021].

Chapman, S. (2019) When caring counts: Fostering empathy and compassion through the arts using animation. In: Barton, G. and Garvis, S. (eds.) *Compassion and Empathy in Educational Contexts.* Switzerland: Palgrave MacMillan.

Cocker, F. and Joss, N. (2016) Compassion fatigue among healthcare, emergency and community service workers: A systematic review. *International Journal of Environmental Research and Public Health*, 13 (6), 618. Available from: doi: 10.3390/ijerph13060618

Colaianne, B., Galla, B. and Roeser R. (2020) Perceptions of mindful teaching are associated with longitudinal change in adolescents' mindfulness and compassion. *International Journal of Behavioral Development*, 44 (1), 41–50.

Columbus, K. (2021) *How to Listen: Tools for Opening up Conversations When it Matters Most*. London: Kyle Books.

Delaney, M. (2009) *Teaching the Unteachable*. London: Worth Publishing.

Department of Health and Social Care (2021a) *Handbook to the NHS Constitution for England*. Available from: https://www.gov.uk/government/publications/supplements-to-the-nhs-constitution-for-england/the-handbook-to-the-nhs-constitution-for-england [Accessed 24th September 2021]. Open Government Licence v3.0 OGL. Full details available at: https://www.nationalarchives.gov.uk/doc/open-government-licence/version/3/

Department of Health and Social Care (2021b) *The NHS Constitution for England*. Available from: https://www.gov.uk/government/publications/the-nhs-constitution-for-england/the-nhs-constitution-for-england [Accessed 24th September 2021]. Open Government Licence v3.0 OGL. Full details available at: https://www.nationalarchives.gov.uk/doc/open-government-licence/version/3/

Dowling, T. (2018) Compassion does not fatigue! *Canadian Veterinary Journal*, 59 (7), 749–750.

Eccles, J. and Roeser, R. (2016) School and community influences on human development. In: Boorstein, M. and Lamb, M. (eds.) *Developmental Science: An Advanced Textbook*. 7th ed. Hillsdale, NJ: Erlbaum. 645–728.

Education Scotland (n.d.) The compassionate and connected classroom curricular resource. Available from: https://education.gov.scot/media/3ugjamia/nih087-compassionate-and-connected-classroom__.pdf [22nd December 2021]. Open Government Licence v3.0 OGL. Full details available at: https://www.nationalarchives.gov.uk/doc/open-government-licence/version/3/

Esch, T. and Stefano, G. (2011) The neurobiological link between compassion and love. *Medical Science Monitor: International Medical Journal of Experimental and Clinical Research*, 17(3), RA65–RA75.

Forsell, L. and Åström, J. (2012) An analysis of resistance to change exposed in individuals' thoughts and behaviors. *Comprehensive Psychology*, January. Available from: https://journals.sagepub.com/doi/full/10.2466/09.02.10.CP.1.17 [Accessed 27th August 2021].

Gerbarg, P., Brown, R., Streeter, C., Katzman, M., and Vermani, M. (2019) Breath practices for survivor and caregiver stress, depression, and post- traumatic stress disorder: Connection, co-regulation, compassion. *OBM Integrative and Complementary Medicine*, 4 (3). Available from: doi: 10.21926/obm.icm.1903045

Gerber, Z. and Anaki, D. (2021) The role of self-compassion, concern for others, and basic psychological needs in the reduction of caregiving burnout. *Mindfulness*, 12, 741–750.

Gerhardt, S. (2004) *Why Love Matters: How Affection Shapes a Baby's Brain*. Hove, East Sussex: Brunner-Routledge.

Gilbert, P. (2021) Creating a compassionate world: Addressing the conflicts between sharing and caring versus controlling and holding evolved strategies. *Frontiers in Psychologyy*, 11, 582090. Available from: doi: 10.3389/fpsyg.2020.582090

Gilbert, P., Catarino, F., Duarte, C. Matos, M., Kolts, R., Stubbs, J., Ceresatto, L, Duarte, J., Pinto-Gouveia, J. and Basran, J. (2017) The development of compassionate engagement and action scales for self and others. *Journal of Compassionate Health Care*, 4 (4). Available from: https://jcompassionatehc.biomedcentral.com/articles/10.1186/s40639-017-0033-3#citeas [Accessed 29th July 2021].

Goetz, J., Keltner, D. and Simon-Thomas, E. (2010) Compassion: An evolutionary analysis and empirical review *Psychological Bulletin*, May 136 (3), 351–374.

Gonzalez-Mendez, R. and Díaz, M. (2021) Volunteers' compassion fatigue, compassion satisfaction, and post-traumatic growth during the SARS-CoV-2 lockdown in Spain: Self-compassion and self-determination as predictors. *PLoS ONE* 16 (9), e0256854. Available from: doi: 10.1371/journal.pone.0256854

Green, D. (2021) University of Sussex teams up with BBC in kindness research. *The Argos*, 2 September. Available from: https://www.theargus.co.uk/news/19554635.university-sussex -teams-bbc-kindness-research/. [Accessed 03rd January 2022].

Halifax, J. (2012). A heuristic model of enactive compassion. *Current Opinion in Supportive and Palliative Care*, 6 (2), 228–235.

Hammond, C. (2021) What we do and don't know about kindness. Available from: https://www .bbc.com/future/article/20210921-what-we-do-and-dont-know-about-kindness [Accessed 12th January 2022].

Hermanto, N. and Zuroff, D. (2016) The social mentality theory of self-compassion and self-reassurance: The interactive effect of care-seeking and caregiving. *Journal of Social Psychology* Available from: https://self-compassion.org/wp-content/uploads/2016/06/Hermanto_2016 .pdf [Accessed 17th June 2021].

Hilppö, J., Rajala, A. and Lipponen, L. (2019) Compassion in Children's peer cultures processes In: Barton, G. and Garvis, S. (eds.) *Compassion and Empathy in Educational Contexts*. Cham, Switzerland: Palgrave McMillan.

Hofmyer, A., Kennedy, K. and Taylor, R. (2020) Contesting the term 'compassion fatigue': Integrating findings from social neuroscience and self-care research. *Collegian*, April, 27 (2), 232–237. Available from: doi: 10.1016/j.colegn.2019.07.001

Lau, B., Chan, C. and Ng S.-M. (2020) Self-compassion buffers the adverse mental health impacts of COVID-19-related threats: Results from a cross-sectional survey at the first peak of Hong Kong's outbreak. *Frontiers in Psychiatry*, 11, 585270. Available from: https://www.frontiersin .org/article/10.3389/fpsyt.2020. [Accessed 30th October 2021].

Lew, A. (2002) Helping children cope in an increasingly threatening world: Four cornerstones of emotional well-being. *The Family Journal: Counseling and Therapy for Couples and Families*, April, 10 (2), 134–138.

Maestri, G. and Monforte, P. (2020) Who deserves compassion? The moral and emotional dilemmas of volunteering in the 'refugee crisis.' *Sociology*, 54 (5), 920–935. Available at: doi: 10.1177/0038038520928199

Mascaro, J.S., Florian, M.P., Ash, M.J., Palmer, P.K., Frazier, T., Condon, P. and Raison, C. (2020) Ways of knowing compassion: How do we come to know, understand, and measure compassion when we see it? *Frontiers in Psychology*, 11. Available from: https://www .frontiersin.org/articles/10.3389/fpsyg.2020.547241/full [Accessed 18th May 2021].

Mental Health Foundation (2020) Why did we pick kindness as the theme? Available from: https://www.mentalhealth.org.uk/campaigns/kindness/why-kindness-theme [Accessed 06th December 2021].

Miralles, A., Raymond, M. and Lecointre, G. (2019) Empathy and compassion toward other species decrease with evolutionary divergence time. *Scientific Reports*, 9, Article no. 19555. Available from: https://www.nature.com/articles/s41598-019-56006-9#citeas [Accessed 03rd January 2022].

Moberg, K.U. (2003) *The Oxytocin Factor: Tapping the Hormone of Calm, Love, and Healing.* Cambridge, MA: Da Capo Press.

National Scientific Council on the Developing Child (2005) *Excessive Stress Disrupts the Architecture of the Developing Brain*. Working Paper #3. Cambridge: Harvard University Press.

Neff, K. (2003) Self-compassion: An alternative conceptualization of a healthy attitude toward oneself. *Self and Identity*, 2 (2), 85–101.

Neff, K. and Seppälä, E. (2017) Compassion, well-being, and the hypo-egoic self. In: Brown, K. and Leary, M. (eds.), *The Oxford Handbook of Hypo-egoic Phenomena: Theory and Research on the Quiet Ego*. Oxford: Oxford University Press. 189–202.

Nilsson, P. (2014) Are empathy and compassion bad for the professional social worker? *Advances in Social Work*, Fall, 15 (2), 294–305.

Nussbaum, M. (1996) Compassion: The basic social emotion. *Social Philosophy and Policy*, 13 (1), 27–58.

Otake, K., Shimai, S., Tanaka-Matsumi, J. Otsui, K. and Fredrckson, B. (2006) Happy people become happier through kindness: A counting kindnesses intervention. *Journal of Happiness Studies*, 7, 361–375.

Peplak, J. and Malti, T. (2021) Toward generalized concern: The development of compassion and links to kind orientations. *Journal of Adolescent Research*. OnlineFirst April. Available from: doi: 10.1177/07435584211007840 [Accessed 22nd May 2022].

Porges, S. (2011) *The Polyvagal Theory: Neurophysiological Foundations of Emotions, Attachment, Communication, Self-regulation*. New York: WW Norton.

Porges, S. (2017) Vagal pathways: Portals to compassion. In: Seppälä, M., Simon-Thomas, M., Brown, S., Worline, M., Cameron, C.D. and Doty, J. (eds.) *The Oxford Handbook of Compassion Science*. New York: Oxford University Press. 189–204.

Preckel, K., Kanske, P. and Singer, T. (2018) On the interaction of social affect and cognition: Empathy, compassion and theory of mind. *Current Opinion in Behavioral Sciences*,19, 1–6.

Schwartz, R. (1997) *Internal Family Systems Therapy*. 1st ed., The Guilford Family Therapy. New York: Guilford Press.

Schwartz, R. (2021) *No Bad Parts: Healing Trauma and Restoring Wholeness with the Internal Family Systems Model*. Boulder: Sounds True Inc.

Schwartz, R. and Sweezy, M. (2019) *Internal Family Systems Therapy*. New York: Guilford Publications.

Shonkoff, J. and Phillips, D. (eds.) (2000) *From Neurons to Neighborhoods: The Science of Early Childhood Development*. Washington, DC: National Academies Press.

Singer, T. and Engert, V. (2019) It matters what you practice: Differential training effects on subjective experience, behavior, brain and body in the ReSource project. *Current Opinion in Psychology*, 28, 151–158.

Smullens, S. (2012) What I wish I had known: Burnout and self-care in our social work profession. The new social worker. Fall. Available from: https://www.socialworker.com/feature-articles /field-placement/What_I_Wish_I_Had_Known_Burnout_and_Self-Care_in_Our_Social _Work_Profession/. [Accessed 18th January 2022].

Šolcová, I., Vinokhodova, A., Gushin, V. and Kuznetsova, P. (2022) Tend-and-befriend behaviour during spaceflight simulation. *Acta Astronautica*, February, 191, 79–87. Available from: doi: 10.1016/j.actaastro.2021.11.001.

Spiegel, L. (2017) *Internal Family systems Therapy with Children*. New York: Routledge.

Stone, L. (2020) Life and times. Rationing the milk of human kindness: The fable of the dun cow. *British Journal of General Practice*, 18 July. Available from: https://bjgplife.com/fable. [Accessed 29th July 201].

Strauss, C., Taylor, B., Gu, J., Kuyken, W., Baer, R., Jones, F. and Cavanagh, K. (2016) What is compassion and how can we measure it? A review of definitions and measures. *Clinical Psychology Review*, 47, 15–27.

Sunderland, M. (2016) *The Science of Parenting*. 2nd ed. London: DK Publishing.

Taylor, S., Klein, L., Lewis, B., Gruenewald, T., Gurung, R. and Updegraff, J. (2000) Biobehavioral responses to stress in females: Tend-and-befriend, not fight-or-flight. *Psychological Review*, 107, 411–429.

Thapa, D., Levett-Jones, T., West, S. and Cleary, M. (2021) Burnout, compassion fatigue, and resilience among healthcare professionals. *Nursing and Health Sciences*, 23, 565–569. Available from: doi: 10.1111/nhs.12843.

Weng, H., Fox, A., Shackman, A., Stodola, D., Caldwell, J., Olson, M., Rogers, G. and Davidson, R. (2013) Compassion training alters altruism and neural responses to suffering. *Psychological Science*, 24, 1171–1180.

Wilkinson, H., Whittington, R., Perry, L. and Eames, C. (2017) Examining the relationship between burnout and empathy in healthcare professionals: A systematic review. *Burnout Research*, September, 6, 18–29.

Williams, B., Lau, R., Thornton, M and Olney, L. (2017) The relationship between empathy and burnout–lessons for paramedics: A scoping review. *Psychology Research and Behavior Management*, 10, 329–337. Available from: https://www.ncbi.nlm.nih.gov/pmc/articles/PMC5708197/#. [Accessed 27th May 2021].

Williams, C. (2008) Compassion, suffering and the self: A moral psychology of social justice. *Current Sociology*, January, 56 (1), 5–24. Available from: doi: 10.1177/0011392107084376

Chapter 4

Containment

Holding it together

Containment is a relationship between parent and child in which the adult manages big feelings for the child and soothes or regulates their emotional state (American Psychological Association, n.d.a). Containment is also referred to as 'holding'. In schools, we create containment, or a 'holding' environment, when we maintain a space where the pupil experiencing dysregulated emotion is safe and soothed by an adult who can manage the strong feelings themselves and can reflect on what is being experienced by the pupil. This can include naming feelings and bodily states in a non-judgemental way, using tone of voice to calm, slowing the pace of the interaction, and offering strategies for cooling down or warming up the pupil's physical (body) and psychological (brain) systems.

Josephine Klein (1987) described containment as the state of an adult emotionally holding a child in order for them to consolidate their experience, illustrating this as being like a wrapping for a glued-together object, holding it together until the glue is adequately set. We would not expect young humans to be able to manage and make sense of anger, anxiety, joy, or excitement in the way older humans may be expected to. The wiser, stronger adult offers a compassionate container for children who are experiencing strong emotions as the sensations register, are lived through, and subside. We wrap our calm around the child until they return to a state of equilibrium, experiencing this calm support from carers means that in time children can hold themselves together without adult support.

The stress of experiencing strong emotions may be good for us. It certainly is in survival terms, when fear motivates action. In everyday terms, the emotions may lead to action that improves our relationships or our lives. Feelings of surviving or managing stress can feel good. Learning we 'come out the other end' of big feelings builds our capacity for resilience. Too much stress, or ongoing unresolved stress, has been found to be bad for us (McEwen, 2012; Patel & Patel, 2019); feelings of emotional overload or of overwhelming fear, anxiety, or anger, have a toll on our bodies as well as our brains. Containing or holding the child experiencing stressful feelings is the role of an adult in early childhood. Adults who can soothe the child and return them to a sense of safety

DOI: 10.4324/9781003277903-5

Containment

and calm are necessary to avoid the corrosive impact of ongoing stress on the developing brain (Bellis et al., 2017).

Window of tolerance

'Window of tolerance' is an important concept, but it can be hard to know how to judge whether the window is breached by the emotions of a pupil (or ourselves). Janina Fisher (2021) offered a helpful framework for gauging whether we are within the window and able to function and manage. We are within our window of tolerance, despite experiencing some levels of discomfort and stretch, when we are able to both think and feel. If we are noticing our brains becoming fuzzy, we can no longer think straight, or our thoughts are confused or not accessible to us, then we are becoming hyper-aroused, and it is time to take a break. When we realise our feelings are 'off-line', and we start to feel numb or distant to ourselves, then we are becoming hypo-aroused and need to change our state. Helping children to recognise physical cues to their mental states is beneficial. Knowing a pupil well enough to gauge their window of tolerance and recognise the signs is more likely when we are familiar with the physical signals that tell us when our brain or body is becoming overwhelmed.

Klein (1987) explained that a young person will be unable to make sense of emotions which appear to be rushing through them. You may remember times when a feeling is so big you wonder if you are about to explode or implode, fragment or disappear. Klein talked of 'holding' as a frame or a scaffold that holds the child within the space, stopping explosions or fragmentations, and preventing collapse or implosion. This slows everything down: the need to act becomes less imperative, time is created to feel the feeling, access the thinking brain, and choose what might be the next action.

The visual picture of containment as a frame or a wrap-around for someone in the midst of feelings that are experienced as overwhelming may be helpful for us. It suggests why staying with pupils experiencing big feelings, soothing the child or young person, and externally processing the experience really matters. Time in with the adult is helpful, while time out alone means no container or external manager to model the process of regulating bodily and emotional states. Time out is appropriate and helpful for pupils who can use this as a strategy and when they feel agency in choosing time out as a positive step in their process of self-regulation; it is not helpful for pupils who, as yet, have no strategies for processing dysregulation, who perceive time out as rejection and abandonment, or who need a supportive other as a containing source of external regulation.

What is emotion?

Emotion may not be clear and simple to define. The *Collins English Dictionary* (n.d.) offers a simple distinction between feelings (emotions) as part of one's character and thoughts as another part. *Collins'* definition notes the interchangeable use in everyday language of 'emotions' and 'feelings'. Other definitions talk about emotions as being the evaluation of external experiences, the brain and body responses, and the behavioural expression of the responses to those evaluations. This suggests that emotions are created through input and expressed by an output.

The Handbook of Human Emotions (Watt Smith, 2015) includes descriptions of around 150 emotions. Jaak Panksepp, a neuroscientist, psychobiologist, and author of *Affective Neuroscience* (2004), categorised emotions into seven primary emotional systems: seeking, care, play, lust, fear, sadness, and anger. This may feel like a big discrepancy in numbers of emotions compared with the views of Watt Smith. Panksepp believed that a wider range of secondary and tertiary emotions can be seen as subsets of his main seven categories. Others have proposed only four basic emotions (Jack et al., 2014) which may combine to form complex or compound emotions. The four are happiness, sadness, fear, and anger.

The theory of emotion links our emotions to our survival needs: feeling good or happy in situations or with people means we will seek out these people and places. This leads to reward chemicals being released in our brains and to the likelihood that we will build connections to these sources of happy feelings. Sadness could be linked to feelings of loss: loss of happiness, loss of sources of happiness. We will avoid behaviours that we link to loss, being punished by rejection, or denial of resources. Fear can inform our avoidant behaviours, while anger can be a driver for action to overcome barriers and challenges (Williams, 2017).

It is important that we recognise that pleasant and unpleasant emotions have an equally important role in our lives. Panksepp (2011, 2010) believed that emotions can impact us in positive or negative ways, but the emotion itself is not good or bad. We avoid feeling sad or stressed because the experiences that elicit those emotions are often dangerous to our emotional, physical, or social well-being. This resonates with the ideas of Sigmund Freud in the 1920s about survival instincts and his beliefs about our drivers throughout life of seeking pleasure while avoiding pain.

Panksepp (2010) wrote that ideas about good and bad feelings, or positive and negative emotions, are our current conceptualisations and not actual states. Basic emotions are about informing our actions that are likely to ensure survival and comfort and, therefore, are all 'good' if good means helpful. The internal states are felt to be good or bad rather than being good or bad (Panksepp, 2011). Without thinking about why we feel what we feel, it may be easy to think of feelings as 'good' or 'bad'. There are emotions we express freely to others and other emotions we hide. We accept, tolerate, or welcome expressions of some emotions from people, while we ignore, discourage, or censor others. We have developed value judgements on emotions. Early family experiences may inform our personal concept of 'good' and 'bad' feelings, as might a wider social and cultural environment. For instance, birth order may have influenced family subliminal messages about positive and negative emotions within the home. If you are the oldest, it may be acceptable to express frustration; if you are the baby of the family, it may be acceptable to be frightened or sad.

We often give messages to children without knowing or meaning to, through our responses or reactions to the expressions of their emotions. Children can internalise this in a more global way:

- I feel anger. Anger is bad. I am bad.
- I feel happy. Happy is good. I am good.

We may unconsciously accept or deny some feelings or approve of and disapprove of others. All of us may recognise feelings of guilt or shame when we feel angry and maybe guilt and inadequacy when we are not feeling happy. Social media can play into our feelings of 'I should be happy' and 'I should not be sad'. We are becoming more aware that it is OK to be sad or angry. We still have some way to go in accepting that it is also OK not to know how you feel or to feel more than one thing at once.

Containment

Mixed emotions

It is helpful to enable children to recognise that they have mixed emotions and to acknowledge that experiencing complex or contrary emotions can feel confusing. Most of our feelings are not completely straightforward. We often have more than one emotion at a time, or an emotion which borders on another emotion, even its opposite. Having emotions which we experience as making us feel good, at the same time as having an internal state that makes us feel bad, is called mixed emotions. They are a common response to complex situations. Feeling excited and anxious all at once is not an uncommon experience.

We do not often stop to reflect more deeply on emotions and the fact we, or a child, may be feeling more than one emotion. Naming emotions has long been recognised as important for children's developing emotional intelligence. It is also a means for containing those emotions by recognising and accepting them. Naming emotions can be straightforward, or it can be complicated. Physical signs of emotion are sometimes universal but can also be influenced by culture and personal experiences.

Giving the name of a definite, discreet emotion that does not fit with the pupil's sense of their own state could make a child feel misunderstood, or sense that we are not in tune with them. Phrases like:

- *big feelings*
- *difficult feelings*
- *mixed-up feelings*

are ways to demonstrate attunement and empathy, without imposing our own frame of reference on a child. We might see clear physical signs that an emotion is present without a clear sense of what that emotion might be. Then we can talk about how the feeling is:

- making your body tense
- making you not want to do anything
- making your head fuzzy.

Thinking about parts

Mixed emotions could be understood through ideas of how we hold different emotions together within our mind and body. Parts psychology talks about different parts of us holding different emotions. The 2015 Disney film *Inside Out* is a visual illustration of different parts competing or working together to guide us through the minefield that is everyday life. Having the language to say that 'part of me is happy about not having to go to the party, but part of me is disappointed' could help me to understand myself better than if I were limited to saying, 'I have mixed emotions', or being restricted to saying, 'I don't know how I feel'. It simplifies complex feelings if I can think, 'the part of me that likes an easy life does not want to challenge someone', and 'the part of me that is passionate about fairness does want to challenge them'. Then I see why I am in a dilemma or why I have mixed emotions.

It could be that talking to pupils in terms of saying 'a part of you is really sad' or 'a part of you feels like giving up' is a way of making feelings more accessible and more manageable. It may also help us to understand why we feel cross with ourselves, or frustrated with our actions and choices. Other parts of us may have different views and want or need different things. While, as adults, it is our job to make sure a child can manage their emotion and, when necessary, step in and help to co-regulate the emotion, it is also our job to fully recognise the sense of enormity of that emotion for a child not to deny it. 'A part of you REALLY wants to rip that page' recognises the depth of the feeling while still recognising another part that knows that the action would lead to consequences.

Cognition and understanding of mental processes help us to feel compassion for ourselves and others.

The part of you that finds it hard to wait rushed in without thinking.

This illustrates how the language of parts could help a child to see a feeling and a following action as understandable while not defining the whole of who they are.

The language of parts, and other ways of contextualising feelings through language, are ways of reframing the enormity of experience and being a helpful presence for our pupils. As well as communicating 'a part of you' feels that, we can also communicate:

- *Right now, you feel angry.*
- *You can't manage such a big feeling on your own yet.*
- *You are still learning how to manage feeling angry.*

Giving a context of time or process helps the pupil to feel that things can change. Understanding may create the belief that the overwhelming feeling is not endless. Paris Goodyear Brown (www.parisgoodyearbrown.com) suggested that, rather than always giving limits and consequences, there are times when we can offer a 're-do' opportunity. 'You are just learning not to shout when you are angry – let's re-do that' is a helpful response when 'don't shout' may feel like an unattainable goal for an overwhelmed child.

What is emotion regulation?

Emotion regulation is the capacity of an individual to manage and modify their emotions (APA, n.d.b). Modifying emotions can be an implicit (unconscious) or explicit (conscious) process (Ahmed et al., 2015; APA, n.d.b). Implicit emotion regulation is the management or change of one's emotional state without awareness of deliberately doing so. This automatic modification of emotion may be deeply learned behaviour from the soothing presence of the external parent figure which has been internalised and 'built' into the wiring of the brain. Explicit emotion regulation occurs when we use techniques and strategies, understand more and think differently about triggers, and know that there are ways to manage and change emotional states. This learning may, again, be from early years experiences of adults processing emotional experiences and naming or describing strategies as they are tried and tested by the young child or young person.

Emotional competence (Denham et al., 2012; Housman, 2017) is described as the regulation of emotional expression and experience, as well as an understanding of emotion in self and in others. Emotional stability describes how effectively the equilibrium of the emotional system of an individual is sustained and the speed and ease with which poise and balance are regained after stability has been lost (Chaturvedi & Chander, 2010). Emotional stability or competence and good ability for emotion regulation are associated with flexibility and adaptation and are frequently linked to optimism. Equanimity and balance are benefits of the ability to regulate emotions, and it is the presentation of genuine calm and composure at times of difficulty and challenge that signal stable, competent skills of emotion regulation. These benefits are influential in many domains of life. Being able to contain or regulate our emotions helps us to sustain activities, relationships, and our sense of ourselves. It means better physical health through avoiding long exposure to damaging stress or reliance on external regulation through unhealthy means such as food, alcohol or risk-taking behaviours.

Seeing emotion regulation as a process, Gross (1998) recognised opportunities for change in the process at each of his identified five stages:

- controlling which situations or environments we are in
- adapting or changing the situation or environment
- where or what we pay attention to
- adapting and developing our understanding
- adapting or developing new responses.

The first two 'stages' of situational context are more accessible the more independent we become – choosing, moving, leaving, avoiding, and controlling situations depend on physical ability to move and control, as well as permission or authority to do so. We can immediately identify how school environments limit opportunities for pupils to engage their initial emotion regulation responses in classroom situations. Knowing we cannot remove ourselves from situations – for example, sitting next to peers or completing work tasks – immediately triggers our emotional responses and moves us up the ladder of emotional intensity, with accompanying physical symptoms of increasing emotional dysregulation.

Golombek et al. (2020) noted that socially anxious children employ avoidance of situations that trigger anxiety and engage in more behaviours that increase the likelihood of feeling safe as strategies for regulating emotions. Avoidance and modification of situations and environments are normal and appropriate strategies when more adaptive, developmentally complex strategies are not yet developed. While classroom life, group needs, and curriculum demands mean we block the flight response in pupils feeling or anticipating emotional dysregulation, we can support the expansion of tolerance of feelings and the development of a wider repertoire of responses when we understand and acknowledge the experience of pupils in the situations which they find difficult.

Frivold Kostøl and Cameron (2020) suggested that as well as giving words for emotions we use tone of voice, empathy, and accurate appraisal of the child's emotional state in order to be the containment of their feelings as they find their own ways to stabilise and regain balance and poise. Ongoing experiences of empathy, feeling heard, being comforted, and being supported to understand and express emotions develops the child's ability to self-regulate (Frivold Kostøl & Cameron, 2020; Sunderland, 2016). When we set classroom tasks or approach times of transition, we often anticipate which pupils need additional emotional support. These are times we can support the development of self-regulation through approaches similar to early parenting practices of 'talking them through it' and mental state talk.

Appraising and attuning to the child might sound like this:

- *It is hard to work in a group – you are practicing group work and finding that it does not feel comfortable yet.*

Containment

- *Part of you is thinking 'what happens if I can't answer the questions?', and that makes having a go feel scary.*
- *Checking out what will happen next helps you feel calmer about moving rooms.*

Another way might involve acknowledging the child's emotion in a gentle and calm voice, using a word or two or a short sentence:

- *Feeling unsure.*
- *Starting a blank page feels scary.*
- *You don't feel ready.*

Demonstrating empathy is similar, but may offer a greater sense of really understanding:

- *Endings and beginnings feel hard. You wish you did not have to have all these changes of room in your day. It means drawing on a lot of your energies to manage. That must be tiring over the school day.*
- *You are frustrated with that piece of work. You feel that you could do better, and it is frustrating to feel it hasn't gone right. I am guessing that feels disappointing and annoying.*
- *My, that is exciting. Now that you have heard about the visitor this afternoon, you can't think about this morning's work. Thinking about maths is so hard when you are feeling jittery and revved up about something happening later.*

Being the safe adult who contains the child as they recover equilibrium is communicated by simple words and actions about the here and now and the near future. Messages are clear and to the point:

- *I am here.*
- *We can take our time.*
- *I'll check in with you again in a minute.*

Emotion regulation is linked to the ability to manage feelings in order to prioritise long-terms gains over immediate gratification (Goodman et al., 2015). This could apply to classroom behaviours in which maturing pupils resist impulses to avoid work, engage with peers, or pick an easy way, and instead choose to apply themselves to their learning, as they appreciate where this could get them in the future. Ahmed et al. (2015) described a model of emotion regulation in which there is a cognitive component of not only being able to identify the emotion or the trigger of the emotion but also understanding that moderating the emotions is helpful, knowing that there are strategies available to effect a helpful change and which strategy is a match for the emotion, the situation, or the intended goal. Giving a running commentary to the emotion, as well as offering empathic understanding to the child, helps to reflect on how the emotion may be caused and what can happen as a result of experiencing that emotion.

Recognising an emotion and linking it to the experience that elicits the emotion could look like this:

- *You feel so angry about not being picked for the team.*
- *You feel sad that Tricia can't come to your party.*

Containment

- *You feel very happy that Sam likes your new boots.*
- *You are not sure yet how you feel about going on the trip.*
- *Part of you wants to play, and part of you is worried you don't know the rules. Having two feelings at once is difficult.*

Acknowledging the pupil's own desire to manage the emotion might look like this:

- *You know that you want to feel calmer. You want to speak to Chelsea and know it will go better if you do not feel so angry.*
- *You know feeling this excited about this evening will make your day hard, and you want to get on with your work so the day will go faster.*

Helping the pupil to consider how managing the emotion could have positive outcomes could look like this:

- *It seems like when you are feeling such a lot of frustration it is impossible to think straight. Feeling less frustrated might mean being able to see a way forward.*
- *Having big feelings means that our thinking brain can't do its job and that makes us feel even more frustrated, which means we can't work out what to do. Less energy for feelings gives more energy for thinking.*

Acknowledging the pupil's own strategies to manage the emotion might look like this:

- *You know what works for you. You are moving away until you feel calmer.*
- *You're not ready to have another go yet. Drawing is a way of changing how you feel that you know works for you.*

Supporting ways of changing emotional states, or the strength of the emotion, and choosing an appropriate strategy can sound like this:

- *Let's think. What might change the way that you feel? Can you remember any help-ful ways that give you space to think?*
- *Do you remember the blu-tack blob? When you squeeze your blu-tack, I remember seeing you squash stress into less.*
- *I'm thinking about square breathing – breathe in while you count to 5. Hold it while you count to 5. Breathe out while you count to 5. Hold it while you count to 5. It might give your brain and body a chance to calm down.*
- *I wonder if telling me a bit more about how you feel might help?*

Different age groups' ability to regulate emotion means different expectations of the regulatory process during early years, latency, and adolescence. Parts of the process emerge early in development but are enhanced and expanded as we mature. While some may feel that the development of the ability to contain and regulate emotions in pre-school age is key to academic achievement and success in work and adult relationships (Fallon et al., 2020), others recognise that adolescence is a further key opportunity for brain change and growth. Toddlerhood, the 'terrible twos', is a stage of substantial development in terms of developing autonomy, risk taking, and forming a sense of indi-viduation and personal identity. This stage is often compared to later turbulent teenage years. Much literature offers understanding of the development of emotion regulation in the early years. Increasingly, interest in emotion regulation in adolescence is leading to research and interventions for this age group.

The ability to identify, choose, and apply strategies consolidates during adolescence (Ahmed et al., 2015). Cognition, or concrete understanding of and the ability to reflect upon, situations and feelings increases. The strategies used to regulate emotions change as the brain develops; the middle stage of adolescence is a particular time of change in the development and use of emotion regulation strategies (Theurel & Gentaz, 2018). The ability to re-appraise events and situations at this age offers new opportunities for supporting the development of emotion regulation skills. Helpful age-appropriate responses to adolescents could sound like this:

- *Can we think about what happened? I wonder if we might check whether you missed something or whether you saw something that maybe wasn't quite how it seemed?*
- *Part of you knew exactly what was going on. I wonder if there is another part of you that is not so sure? What might that other part have to say about what happened?*
- *You say your head was ringing by then. That must have made it hard to hear what was being said. When our body has gone into 'fight or flight' mode, we are programmed to notice threat and danger or the possibility of any kind of harm, and not to see or hear if there is help from someone or even if the person who we feel threatened by has started to back down. When the ringing has stopped it is a good time to 'rewind' and think again about how what happened is not always the same as how it felt at the time.*

The Organisation for Economic Co-operation and Development (OECD, n.d.) undertook a survey of social and emotional skills in 10- and 15-year-olds. They reported that gains in emotional stability in pre-adolescence regress during adolescence before recovering post-adolescence. Emotion regulation is a work in progress; as the brain matures new capabilities come online. In secondary settings, pupils are more able to evaluate their emotional experiences. They may be mature enough to think about the feeling and reflect on why they feel it. Older students may have developed the ability to consider whether the feeling is appropriate to the situation. Time spent reflecting and evaluating leads to an opportunity to choose what happens next. Adolescents are also navigating other important developmental tasks; these take much of their focus and energies, meaning self-regulation skills decrease. Skills need exercising, and adolescents may respond to creative ways to practice self-regulation. Drama and role play can offer some level of emotional experience when 'playing out' scenarios in which emotions are recognised and altered for students in Key Stage 3 and 4.

A review of the importance of social and emotional skills by Goodman et al. (2015) for the Early Intervention Foundation listed five main skills for social and emotional well-being. The report concluded that self-regulation is the most important life-skill for us to foster if we are to have a positive overall sense of satisfaction with our lives. Sometimes, people with poorly developed emotional regulation skills are described as immature, reckless, selfish, volatile, and intolerant. People with well-regulated emotions appear mature, measured, considerate, tolerant, and calm. The risks of not developing emotion regulation skills include the possibility of being unable to inhibit our damaging behaviours. This could mean we damage our chances of social inclusion, our physical health, and our academic engagement (Goodman et al., 2015). There is a reciprocal

Containment

relationship – poorly regulated pupils may be rejected by peers, and social exclusion can lead to poor self-regulation (Stenseng et al., 2014).

Attachment relationships and emotion regulation

Think about a baby who is surprised, scared, or not sure, and is just about to cry. The baby looks at the adult and the adult pulls a (relatively) scared face, then smiles and makes soothing noises. Without training, parents naturally attune to the feeling and acknowledge it, not denying it, but making it small enough to be manageable, parcel it up in an attuned, empathic response and return it to the child with an unspoken belief: you managed being scared – you are strong enough, and I am here. This is then internalised into the child's beliefs about the world:

- things are not THAT bad
- I can manage this
- someone will be there if I need help.

A good ability to regulate emotions is associated with secure attachment in children. Abtahi and Kerns (2017) suggested that securely attached children spent less time feeling dysregulated when experiencing challenging emotions; through regulating their emotions they have more time and energy to focus on the work tasks in hand. Insecurely attached children may seek external regulation from others, become dysregulated more quickly, and stay dysregulated for longer. Externalising insecurely attached children's behaviours can lead to the teacher being engaged with one student for significant periods of time while peers are disrupted and lessons are interrupted. Other insecurely attached children who internalise their dysregulation can give up on tasks, withdraw from others, or appear to comply and be 'fine' as a way to hide their discomfort and fear.

Avoidant children and young people (CYP), as the name suggests, avoid seeking help so as not to risk rejection or angry responses; anxious CYP seek contact from others and want to keep others close (Marvin et al., 2002). Insecurely attached pupils may also 'avoid' the emotion by denying or suppressing it. One study found that insecurely attached adolescents were dysregulated when experiencing anger and that some suppress or deny sadness (Brenning & Braet, 2013). Attachment behaviours are developed early in life as ways to get, and keep, needed attention or avoid and minimise attention experienced as frightening or dangerous (Brenning & Braet, 2013). Getting away and having time out, or seeking connection and time in, may meet the attachment needs of the dysregulated pupil. Many researchers identify the link between attachment and emotion regulation. In 2020, Gardner et al. published a study of young adults which involved self-reported experiences of emotion regulation/dysregulation. They found that insecure attachment was related to higher emotional dysregulation. The study highlighted that this emotional dysregulation led to more social exclusion, depression, and anxiety.

Social relationships, particularly early attachment relationships, play a major role in setting emotion regulation capabilities. Other factors influence its development, such as:

- temperament
- cognitive development
- sibling relationships
- family beliefs

70

- and, in particular, the quality of the relationship between parents or carers (Lindblom et al., 2016; Morris et al., 2007; Rothbart & Sheese, 2007).

Later, positive regulating relationships can develop emotion regulation for those who have not had enough early support for their self-regulation to mature.

Relationships in school and emotion regulation

The stage of emotion regulation skills we achieve at adulthood is complex and mature (hopefully, all things being well). As adults, we often have more access to an understanding of our motivation and to the 'what' and 'why' of the way we are feeling. We have had time to develop and practice a range of strategies for managing our feelings and have the cognitive ability to reflect on the effectiveness, or otherwise, of those strategies. As adults, we are in a position where we have responsibility for regulating our own emotions, and we have responsibility and opportunity for regulating the emotions of younger people in our care. Teachers may or may not be aware of the impact of their own emotions on their pupils; managing our own emotions and containing emotions in the classroom are helpful abilities. Teachers who are effective regulators of their own emotions and support emotion regulation in their pupils provide for effective practice in the classroom and pupils who feel motivated to engage and to learn (Taxer & Gross, 2018).

Teachers may seek to increase or decrease their own emotion in order to feel better or to work better. They also externally regulate the emotions of their pupils in order for them to 'feel better' and 'perform better'. In our reflection on important psychological areas of life in schools, it is important to consider teachers alongside pupils. This is both to try to address well-being across whole school populations and also to acknowledge that relationships between staff and pupils are hugely impactful, and adults have a responsibility to be aware of the theory that informs positive classroom relationships and practice as well as self-awareness of their own needs and ways of being that influence how they work and who they are.

Teachers may act in ways that project positive energies they may not be feeling, or hide and disguise low mood or anger they are experiencing. These strategies can be used in order to better perform in their educating role, to create more feelings of safety and acceptance for their pupils, or simply to 'get through the day'. Whether to effectively educate (Harris, 1977), entertain while educating (Tauber et al., 1993), build a teacher identity (Hanning, 1984), or create a consistent presentation of positive affect to pupils (Smith & Hansen, 1972), acting to enhance communication in the classroom is recognised as part of our skill set. Hanning (1984) recognised the dichotomy of knowing it is important to 'be yourself' and understanding the role of choosing to be a person who is an effective and engaging communicator. Authenticity and congruence are recognised as being important in therapeutic relationships. We are less likely to 'act' in one-to-one interactions and more liable to 'act' when looking out at a large group of expectant faces, when we want to impart knowledge in a memorable way, while managing behaviour effectively for the benefit of all. This is congruent with being our teacher selves.

Managing behaviours is a part of the teaching role for which teachers may feel they need, and use, their emotion regulation skills and strategies (Taxer & Gross, 2018). Teachers reported suppressing their feelings was a frequently used strategy

Containment

when needing to manage behaviours. Being able to manage our emotions in order to manage our classrooms and learning environments is important (Hagenauer, & Volet, 2014). Teachers model that asking for and expecting appropriate behaviours need not include being punitive, aggressive, upset, or intolerant. Being calm and suppressing feelings of frustration and anger in order to maintain our professional role and to protect our pupils may come at a cost to our physical, emotional, and social well-being (Patel & Patel, 2019; University of Texas at Austin, 2011). We may feel that suppressing our emotions is the appropriate and safe option when employing our classroom management practices. Modelling appropriate behaviours is important, and modelling suppression of feeling needs judicious consideration. Finding a balance between being genuine and being professional is no easy task. Considering the value of emotion regulation and the importance of modelling healthy relationships presents a dilemma when strategies we use may negatively impact us. There may be no easy answer to balancing pupil and teacher well-being, but acknowledging the issue leads to seeking solutions.

It really matters for teachers to have the information that could influence their choices in managing their feelings in ways that support their own mental and physical health. Finding safe, appropriate outlets for suppressed emotions is key – physical activity, time spent in nature, and talking to friends and family may be some of our preferred strategies. Supervision in school would be a powerful way to address the effects of emotion suppression; it also would help to uncover all the times we had not even realised we were acting OK when we really were not feeling OK. Understanding the reasons behind pupil 'mistaken behaviours' reduces staff responses of strong uncomfortable or painful emotions. Supporting pupils' mental health using skills described in this chapter can reduce the strength and length of emotional responses in pupils, again, positively impacting staff emotional experiences and reducing the need for suppression. Supporting the development of our students' own emotion regulation skills could take away some of the pressure we are under for being the external regulator of pupils at the same time we are managing our own feelings.

Enhancing emotion regulation in the classroom

It is likely that emotion regulation in the classroom leads to positive education outcomes (Fried, 2011). Perry and Dobson (2013) suggested that we best support the development of emotion regulation when a child is actually experiencing dysregulation. Noticing and naming emotions, as well as learning to manage emotions, is facilitated 'in the heat of the moment' as the child is experiencing intense and hard to manage emotions. This is very different to Social and Emotional Learning (SEL) programmes in which learning is timetabled and more abstract in nature. Putting knowledge into the thinking brain (using planned teaching for calm children) is giving students helpful resources. Working with the emotional brain in times of arousal is giving students felt experiences for their body to remember. Passing the theory element of your driving test is important; passing the practical element demonstrates you know what to do and that you can put knowledge into safe action on the road. Unlike Perry and Dobson (2013), Fried stated that pro-active calming strategies work better than when responding to already aroused students.

Important elements of classroom experiences which develop pupils' resilience to distress and ability to regulate emotion include:

- staff who model using strategies for emotion regulation
- practices that provide the language for emotions and feelings

talking about how our brains and bodies respond or react to emotional arousal
- encouraging curiosity – 'why' we feel the way that we do
- encouraging creativity – 'how' we can express emotions safely and appropriately, 'how' we can learn to change our emotional states, and 'how' we learn to live with the range of emotions in challenging times.

Learning from the development of emotion regulation in healthy early attachment relationships, we can adapt and adopt key features of parenting responses for use in relationships in school. Morris et al. (2007) explained that parents unintentionally use emotion coaching with their children – a helping skill we can develop for the classroom.

The helpful parenting behaviours we could incorporate into our practice include:

- offering containment
- recognising a child's emotion
- helping the child develop language of emotions
- validating feelings
- demonstrating empathy
- allowing or supporting the child to find their own solutions.

These practices allow children to develop their strategies and skills for regulating feelings. Talking about feelings and listening to pupils to really hear their experiences can support them as they find ways to regulate their feelings and manage emotions that challenge their sense of safety and control.

Acknowledging feelings

Giving words to our feelings results in better physical and mental health (Lieberman et al., 2011); talking about feelings is therapeutic. Giving words to feelings transforms emotions by bringing the thinking brain online (McLaughlin & Holliday, 2013). Overwhelming feelings that might be experienced as unspeakable or shameful are tamed by being given a name and can be acknowledged and then regulated by thinking about them. Lieberman et al. (2011) believed that naming feelings is helpful for engaging our thinking brain and that using language can put the brakes on our emotional brain where the feelings are experienced. Naming feelings to help children regulate their emotions is a 'top-down' intervention, using your higher order brain (thinking) to calm your older emotional brain (feeling). SEL programmes in schools are 'top-down' methods, explicitly teaching strategies and having conversations in which emotional responses are normalised for the child or young person.

In the classroom, we often need children to behave in pro-social ways in which we may encourage denial or suppression of emotions, excitement, anger, fear, and joy, in order for classroom work to continue. Not denying that an emotion exists, and not judging it as negative, while giving limits or acceptable alternatives to its expression is a healthy model of managing emotions appropriately for the context. When we learn new skills for acknowledging and validating emotions whilst giving limits to their expression, we can at least avoid some of the detriments of emotion suppression.

Minimalising experiences, dismissing anxieties, and deflecting the communication of a child who is overwhelmed are understandable strategies in busy classrooms. These strategies are sticking plasters to the problem, designed for the moment, without

Containment

addressing underlying issues or gaps in a student's self-regulation repertoire. The British Psychological Society (BPS, 2020) advised us not to placate pupils with glib platitudes, such as 'don't worry', as this could convey to pupils that we have not truly heard them or taken their experience seriously.

Strategies of ignoring or trying to bury emotions are unhelpful to us when they become our main coping approach or when we are unaware that we do this. Acknowledging the validity and the positive intention of the emotion is helpful. Emotions communicate or want to communicate. When we acknowledge an emotion, we try to listen to the communication, this can calm the feeling (NHS Fife, 2016; Sunderland, 2016; Woolf, 2016). When someone is knocking on the door, you might want to ignore or avoid them, but they will probably knock louder to gain your attention.

If we ignore children who are trying to communicate their emotions to us, often, they will keep trying, and this can mean an escalation of their attempts and of their need to be heard. Although it may sound challenging, allowing students to express their emotions can lead to fewer emotional outbursts. As the adult external manager of emotions, it is possible to safely and appropriately make allowances for some emotional expression while re-directing pupils to acceptable alternatives. The person knocking on your door may keep returning, knocking louder, for longer, and appearing more and more frequently until you finally respond to their need to tell you what it is they need you to hear. Or they may not return, and you will never know what they wanted to see you about.

Conclusion

In schools we are, by default, the early intervention team, and increasing our knowledge and skills can enhance our ability as helpers and facilitators of healthy development. For pupils who have carers at home who are unable to regulate their child's emotions, often because they experience so much dysregulation themselves, a teacher who is emotionally regulated will be experienced as calming and soothing (BPS, 2020). There are many helping skills we can employ in order to support the mental health of CYP by developing their emotion regulation:

- really listening to pupils
- naming feelings and encouraging students to name their feelings
- empathising with feelings
- sharing our own regulating strategies with students and modelling them in class
- emotion coaching
- re-framing emotions in terms of parts of self
- thinking of regulating emotions in terms of a developing process.

Emotions impact behaviours, relationships, ability to concentrate, and motivation for learning. This, then, impacts academic achievement. Safely and supportively managing pupils' emotions, when necessary, while developing pupils' ability to regulate their own emotions whenever possible, are vital skills for staff in schools. Teachers are essential for supporting emotional regulation, particularly for those pupils who lack relationships at home that fulfil this function. Lavy and Eshet (2018) noted that good ability to regulate their own emotions leads to increased job satisfaction and decreased incidents of burnout for staff in schools. Cognition of the theory of emotion regulation, and containment of emotion in practice, can improve the lives of pupils and teachers alike.

> **REFLECTION TASK 3: PERSONAL RESPONSES TO EMOTIONS**
>
> Make a list of emotions and see if, unbidden, you have an immediate reaction to any as good or bad, positive or negative, to be encouraged or suppressed.
>
> Which emotions 'trigger' you?
>
> Imagine a pupil was experiencing each of the emotions in your list. For which emotions would you feel you needed to distract, soothe, or alter their emotional state?
>
> *For instance:*
>
> *If we are 'fixers' or rescuers, we may feel triggered by sadness.*
>
> *If we are easily drawn into a position of 'victim' or need to resolve conflicts, we may be triggered by anger.*
>
> How would you support pupils' development of these three important abilities in the steps to emotion regulation?
>
> * recognising the emotion or the experience that elicits emotion
> * recognising it is necessary or helpful to manage the emotion
> * creating ways of changing the emotional state or the strength of the emotion and choosing an appropriate strategy for the moment.

References

Abtahi, M. and Kerns, K. (2017) Attachment and emotion regulation in middle childhood: Changes in affect and vagal tone during a social stress task. *Attachment and Human Development*, 19 (3), 221–242.

Ahmed, S., Bittencourt-Hewitt, A. and Sebastian, C. (2015) Neurocognitive bases of emotion regulation development in adolescence. *Developmental Cognitive Neuroscience*, 15, 11–25.

American Psychological Association (APA) (n.d.a) Containment. Available at: https://dictionary .apa.org/containment. [Accessed 22nd December 2021].

American Psychological Association (APA) (n.d.b) Emotion regulation. Available from: https:// dictionary.apa.org/emotion-regulation [Accessed 22nd December 2021].

Bellis, M., Hardcastle, K., Ford, K., Hughes, K., Ashton, K., Quigg, Z. and Butler, N. (2017) Does continuous trusted adult support in childhood impart life-course resilience against adverse childhood experiences: A retrospective study on adult health-harming behaviours and mental well-being. *BMC Psychiatry*, 17 (110). Available from: doi: 10.1186/s12888-017-1305-3

Brenning, K. and Braet, C. (2013) The emotion regulation model of attachment: An emotion-specific approach. *Personal Relationships*, 20, 107–123.

British Psychological Society (BPS) (2020) *Emotionally Regulate before We Educate: Focusing on Psychological Wellbeing in the Approach to a New School Day*. Leicester: BPS.

Chaturvedi, M. and Chander, R. (2010) Development of emotional stability scale. *Indian Psychiatry*, Jan-Jun., 19 (1), 37–40.

Collins (n.d.) Collins english dictionary: Emotion. Available from: https://www.collinsdictionary .com/dictionary/english/emotion [Accessed 28th July 2021].

Denham, S., Bassett, H., Way, E., Mincic, M., Zinsser, K. and Graling, K. (2012) Preschoolers' emotion knowledge: Self-regulatory foundations, and predictions of early school success. *Cognition and Emotion*, 26 (4), 667–679.

Fallon, B., Jenkins, J., Conklin Akbari, S. and Joh-Carnella, N. (2020) Abuse, neglect, and maltreatment of infants. In: Benson, J. (ed.) *Encyclopedia of Infant and Early Childhood Development*. 2nd ed. New York: Elsevier.

Fisher, J. (2021) *Transforming the Living Legacy of Trauma: A Workbook for Survivors and Therapists*. Eau Claire: PESI Publishing and Media.

Freud, S. (1920) *Beyond the Pleasure Principle, Group Psychology and Other Works. The Standard Edition of the Complete Psychological Works of Sigmund Freud*, Vol. 18. London: Vintage.

Fried, L. (2011) Teaching teachers about emotion regulation in the classroom. *Australian Journal of Teacher Education*, 36 (3). Available from: doi: 10.14221/ajte.2011v36n3.1 [Accessed 22nd May 2022].

Frivold Kostøl, E. and Cameron, D. (2020) Teachers' responses to children in emotional distress: A study of co-regulation in the first year of primary school in Norway. *Education 3-13*, 49 (7), 821–831.

Gardner, A., Zimmer-Gembeck, M. and Campbell, S. (2020) Attachment and emotion regulation: A person-centred examination and relations with coping with rejection, friendship closeness, and emotional adjustment. *British Journal of Developemental Psychology*, 38, 125–143.

Golombek, K., Lidle, L., Tuschen-Caffier, B., Schmitz, J. and Vierrath, V. (2020) The role of emotion regulation in socially anxious children and adolescents: A systematic review. *European Child & Adolescent Psychiatry*, 29 (11), 1479–1501.

Goodman, A., Joshi, H., Nasim B. and Tyler C. (2015) *Social and Emotional Skills in Childhood and Their Long-term Effects on Adult Life*. London: Institute of Education.

Gross, J. (1998) The emerging field of emotion regulation: An integrative review. *Review of General Psychology*, 2 (3), 271–299.

Hanning, R. (1984) The classroom as theater of self: Some observations for beginning teachers. *ADE Bulletin*, 77, 33–37.

Harris, R. (1977) The teacher as actor. *Teaching of Psychology*, 4 (4), 185–187.

Hagenauer, G. and Volet, S. (2014) "I don't hide my feelings, even though I try to": Insight into teacher educator emotion display. *Australian Educational Researcher*, 41 (3), 261–281. Available from: doi: 10.1007/s13384-013-0129-5

Housman, D. (2017) The importance of emotional competence and self-regulation from birth: A case for the evidence-based emotional cognitive social early learning approach. *ICEP* 11 (13). Available from: doi: 10.1186/s40723-017-0038-6 [Accessed 22nd May 2022].

Inside Out (2015) [film] Pixar, Walt Disney Pictures.

Jack, R., Garrod, O. and Schyns, P. (2014) Dynamic facial expressions of emotion transmit an evolving hierarchy of signals over time. *Current Biology*, 24 (2), 187–192.

Klein, J. (1987) *Our Need for Others and its Roots in Infancy*. London: Routledge.

Lavy, S. and Eshet, R. (2018) Spiral effects of teachers' emotions and emotion regulation strategies: Evidence from a daily diary study. *Teaching and Teacher Education*, 73, 151–161.

Lieberman, M., Inagaki, T., Tabibnia, G. and Crockett, M. (2011) Subjective responses to emotional stimuli during labeling, reappraisal, and distraction. *Emotion*, 11 (3), 468–480.

Lindblom, J., Punamäki, R.-L., Flykt, M., Vänskä, M., Nummi, T., Sinkkonen, J., Tiitinen, A. and Tulppala, M. (2016) Early family relationships predict Children's emotion regulation and defense mechanisms. *SAGE Open*. Available from: doi: 10.1177/2158244016681393

Marvin, R., Cooper, G., Hoffman, K. and Powell, B. (2002) The circle of security project: Attachment-based intervention with caregiver–pre-school child dyads. *Attachment & Human Development*, 4 (1), 107–124.

McEwen, B. (2012) Brain on stress: How the social environment gets under the skin. *PNAS*, 109 (supplement 2), 17180–7185. Available from: https://www.pnas.org/content/109/Supplement _2/17180.full [Accessed 08th July 2021].

McLaughlin, C. and Holliday, C. (2013) *Therapy with Children and Young People: Integrative Counselling in Schools and Other Settings.* London: Sage.

Morris, A., Silk, J., Steinberg, L. Myers, S. and Robinson, L. (2007) The role of the family context in the development of emotion regulation. *Social Development*, 16 (2), 361–388.

NHS Fife (2016) Emotion regulation: Managing emotions. Available from: https://www.moodcafe.co.uk/media/15343/ER_handout_Final_16_June_2016%20pdf.pdf. [Accessed 24th September 2021].

Organisation for Economic Co-operation and Development (OECD) (n.d.) Social and emotional skills, well-being, connectedness and success. Available from: https://www.oecd.org/education/school/UPDATED%20Social%20and%20Emotional%20Skills%20-%20Well-being,%20connectedness%20and%20success.pdf%20(website).pdf. [Accessed 24th September 2021].

Panksepp, J. (2004) *Affective Neuroscience: The Foundations of Human and Animal Emotions (Series in Affective Science).* New York: Oxford University Press.

Panksepp J. (2010) Affective neuroscience of the emotional BrainMind: Evolutionary perspectives and implications for understanding depression. *Dialogues in Clinical Neuroscience*, 12 (4), 533–545.

Panksepp, J. (2011) Cross-species affective neuroscience decoding of the primal affective experiences of humans and related animals. *Plos One.* Available from: https://journals.plos.org/plosone/article?id=10.1371/journal.pone.0021236. [Accessed 3rd October 2021].

Patel, J. and Patel, P. (2019) Consequences of repression of emotion: Physical health, mental health and general well being. *International Journal of Psychotherapy Practice and Research*, 1 (3), 16–21.

Perry, B. and Dobson, C. (2013) The neurosequential model (NMT) in maltreated children. In: Ford, J. and Courtois, C. (eds.) *Treating Complex Traumatic Stress Disorders in Children and Adolescents.* New York: Guilford Press. 249–260.

Rothbart, M., and Sheese, B. (2007) Temperament and emotion regulation. In: Gross, J. J. (ed.) *Handbook of Emotion Regulation.* New York: The Guilford Press. 331–350.

Smith, R. and Hansen, J. (1972) The teacher/actor. *The Clearing House*, 47 (2), 96–98.

Stenseng, F., Belsky, J., Skalicka, V. and Wichstrøm, L. (2014) Social exclusion predicts impaired self-regulation: A 2-year longitudinal panel study including the transition from preschool to school. *Journal of Personality*, 83 (2), 212–220. Available from: doi: 10.1111/jopy.12096.

Sunderland, M. (2016) *The Science of Parenting.* 2nd ed. London: DK Publishing.

Tauber, R., Sargent Mester, C. and Buckwald, S. (1993) The teacher as actor: Entertaining to educate. *NASSP Bulletin*, 77 (551), 20–28.

Taxer, J. and Gross, J. (2018) Emotion regulation in teachers: The "why" and "how". *Teaching and Teacher Education*, 74, 180–189.

Theurel, A. and Gentaz, E. (2018) The regulation of emotions in adolescents: Age differences and emotion-specific patterns. *PLOS ONE* 13(6): e0195501. Available from: doi: 10.1371/journal.pone.0195501

University of Texas at Austin (2011) Psychologists find the meaning of aggression: 'Monty Python' scene helps research. *ScienceDaily*, 24 March. Available from: www.sciencedaily.com/releases/2011/03/110323105202.htm. [Accessed 09th May 2021].

Watt Smith, T. (2015) *The Handbook of Human Emotions.* London: Welcome Collection.

Williams, R. (2017) Anger as a basic emotion and its role in personality building and pathological growth: The neuroscientific, developmental and clinical perspectives. *Frontiers in Psychology*, 8. Available from: doi:10.3389/fpsyg.2017.01950 [Accessed 22nd May 2022].

Woolf, A. (2016) *Better Play: Practical Strategies for Supporting Play in Schools for Children of All Ages.* Belper, Derbyshire: Worth Publishing.

Chapter 5

Connection

Connection is key to human health and well-being

Humans are essentially social animals. We are pre-programmed to seek and form social connection. Our brains are wired to connect and belong (Di Nicola, 2019; Klein, 1987; Lieberman, 2015; Sorel, 2019; Sunderland, 2016; Winnicott, 1974). Feelings and experiences of connection in schools support mental well-being (Allen et al., 2021; Baumeister & Robson, 2021; Pittman & Richmond, 2007; St-Amand et al., 2017). Connection may act as a buffer against burnout in helping profession-als (Gerber & Anaki, 2021). Warmth in interactions and attuned responsiveness to individual students, which sounds a lot like compassion, are elements that support the building of connected classrooms and bonding to school (Jennings & Greenberg, 2009). Associated outcomes of a sense of belonging, such as reductions in conflict and disruptions in the classroom, can also support feelings of ease and calm in the class-room (Jennings & Greenberg, 2009).

Connection refers to a relationship or link between things, places, or people. Social relationships, our connections to others, matter throughout life. As adults, we are famil-iar with the health advice, 'don't smoke', 'avoid obesity', and 'exercise', but we rarely hear 'stay connected to others' in order to stay well. In terms of longevity in humans, the benefits of social relationships may be the same as the benefits of not smoking and more beneficial than exercise or avoiding obesity (Holt-Lunstead et al., 2010). Physical effects of positive social relationships include helpful changes in the way our body responds to stress (Kikusui et al., 2006). Positively relating to others appears to reduce the harmful impacts of cortisol, support stronger immune responses, decrease harmful inflamma-tory responses, may lower blood pressure, and protect against cardiovascular disease (Ford et al., 2019; Umberson & Montez, 2010).

Experiencing connection, like experiencing compassion and containment, has posi-tive biological impacts on our brains and bodies. The effects of social support on cortisol production may offer positive protection against heart and circulation damage from stress (Berkman, 1995; Kikusui et al., 2006). Findings from medical research appear to support the biological function of social supportive relationships in physi-cal health outcomes. Sociology research points to changes in health-supporting and

DOI: 10.4324/9781003277903-6

Connection

health-detrimental behaviours through the quality and quantity of social relationships we do or do not have (Umberson & Montez, 2010). Social connection can be important for safety and engaging with others can change our physical state (Porges, 2009). Kikusui et al. (2006) hypothesised that the presence of social support may mean we feel less vulnerable in some situations. What effects we may gain from social relationships at times of stress is a complex question that requires far more research (Holt-Lunstad, 2021; Smith & Weihs, 2019). We need to know more to understand more, but a link between social connectedness and health, in particular resilience to stress, is increasingly recognised.

Attachment: a template for connection

We may think of positive attachment as love – the safe, warm care that lets us know we are valued. Attachment relationships are not all warm and positive; they are the relationships we grow committed to and reliant on, as they support our survival, whether through comfort, fear, security, uncertainty, calm or chaos.

Attachment theory is a way of looking at important early relationships that we need in order to survive. From birth, connection to others is fundamental to survival and well-being. In order to survive, we innately strive to engage our carer to ensure we are protected and nurtured. In order to survive and thrive, we all had a core early need to be attached to someone who, at best, believes us to be uniquely special or, at least, meets our basic survival needs. Later, these attachment relationships are expanded by new ones. Our first relationships create a map of how relationships work. The map looks a bit like:

- *You are there, I am here, and this is how things happen between us.*

Early experiences may teach us pathways to predicting what happens. Our developing map could look something like this:

- *I am hungry. You feed me.*
- *I am thirsty. You never come.*
- *I am scared. You cannot help me.*
- *I am anxious. You calm me down.*

Later relationships help us to construct more detail on the map:

- *I am sad. Some people help me; others do not help.*
- *I am proud. No one is proud with me.*
- *I am angry. Everyone else is angry.*
- *I am ashamed. Some people think this is funny.*

When our early relationships or attachments are positive, they support our growth and development. Less healthy and nurturing attachment relationships mean that, early in life, we have to adapt to survive; we become who, or what, we need to be in order to get by in life. Later, being the person that we had to be, we can be limited in our ability to develop to our full potential or to experience a sense of fulfilment and meaning in life

Connection

(Klein, 1987; Rogers, 1995; Winnicott, 1974). Attachment relationships can be transactional, which might be through processes such as:

- *If I look after you, you will look after me.*
- *If I smile, you will love me.*
- *If I scream, you will leave me alone.*

Experiences of conditional care and intrusive or dangerous care may lead to a child developing strategies which reflect their understanding that:

- *love is conditional*
- *I can gain safety by my behaviours*
- *I alone am in charge of my destiny.*

Attachment theory specifically refers to carer–child relationships in early life, and other terms, such as para-attachment or allo-attachment, refer to important relationships, particularly when helpful and reparative, outside of the immediate family or care setting. Relationships in schools are important, as teachers are early significant others outside of close family and friendship groups. Klein (1987) explained that our map of how we relate to others becomes clearer and more defined as we experience connections to more people but that the underlying map may remain resistant to change. It is helpful to experience different relationships which offer new learning and a chance for understanding that relationships are not all the same. It can, though, be confusing if ways of relating do not fit your map of expectations. We teachers in schools can remember that change takes time, consistency develops trust, and believing in a world that is safe and kind is a big stretch when, for years, this has not been the map by which life was navigated. Not only do new connections in the brain need to be formed but also tried and tested connections and ways of relating, which previously served the pupil well, have to be put on hold to allow for new ways of understanding to lead to new ways of connecting with us and the environment we create.

Attachment behaviours

In our classrooms, some of the behaviours we find most challenging to manage might be referred to as attachment behaviours. Our 'compliant' students, pupils who want to please us and children who disappear into the group, may also be exhibiting attachment behaviours. Attachment behaviours can reflect positive attachments as well as more challenging ones. Our children and young people (CYP) who are calm, balanced, engaged, motivated, and get on well with peers and adults are also playing out attachment templates, but these are secure attachment behaviours. These pupils developed in a world where others are safe and welcoming. Attachment behaviours reflecting more insecure attachment maps can often be observed as ways that the pupil may bring, or keep, an adult close, or keep distance between themselves and others. Some pupils may rarely need to do either, their attachment 'style' being one of a belief that they count, are capable and courageous, and that, if, or when, they need something, others will be there for connection (Lew, 2002).

There are two attachment systems at work in any interaction between two people, and the adult–child relationship in school is an example of this. Our self-awareness

81

Connection

is important in any work with others. If we can look at our own attachment, it makes us more likely to be helpful to others. In order to be open and available to our pupils when they require helpful responses for their attachment needs, we need to face the challenge of reflecting on our own attachment experiences and the behaviours and relationship patterns that are the results of our own early relationships and environments.

While theory talks about secure or insecure attachment, our attachment state may lie somewhere between the two. This can be experienced as:

At some times, in some places, with some people, I feel safe and able to be myself

while

with others and in different environments, I feel anxious or unable to be myself.

These feelings may tell us to do the things we always do to help us feel safer, like leave, distance ourselves from people, or try and engage people and get closer to them. Or we may not feel the cues are as clear, meaning we may not be sure whether to stay or go, engage or defend. Cognition of attachment theory and of our own life map helps us to feel compassion for ourselves and for others. Acceptance of 'it is what it is' can change how we feel and respond, while 'maybe it could be different' means we may have courage to try out new ways of being or relating.

Attachment and loss

Attachment and loss are experiences that go together. Without attachment, you do not feel loss. Connection to others, feeling attached, caring, and wanting to be with others means that there is then a risk of losing this connection. Children and adults have strong reactions to the threat of loss, and we can see some pupil behaviours through the lens of fear of loss:

- *Children may protect themselves from rejection by avoiding the risk – If I don't care I cannot feel loss.*
- *Children may protect themselves through control or vigilance of important others: – If I keep close, I won't get lost, or you cannot leave me.*

When we care about someone, we feel 'loss' or 'lost' when we are parted from them. In the 1920s, John Bowlby started the conversation about attachment and loss. Bowlby's (1982, 1973) stages of reaction to separation and loss were, at the time he identified them, seen as sequential. Now we see grief as a much less linear process, going in and out and returning to stages in a unique individual experience. Responses to the loss of an attachment figure include protest, despair, and detachment. Expressions of these responses may look like anger, sadness, or denial of feelings.

These three expressions are often seen in the classroom when stress triggers one of these responses, a subconscious return to difficult, even overwhelming, feelings from the past. It is more about an underlying state being exposed than being a reaction to the events in class. We see behaviours and may not recognise their underlying origins. A student becoming upset over a snapped pencil can be seen as 'out of all proportion'.

82

Feeling something has gone wrong, that life seems unfair and that even resources let you down, can trigger memories of much bigger challenging life events. Understanding this process can be helpful in containing our feelings about how we see pupils' responses and how we respond to their feelings (McCrory, 2021; Woolf, 2016). With deeper understanding and new cognition, instead of responses like:

It's only a pencil!
Why is everything always such a big deal for you?
Go and get another one and get on with your work.

we might start to notice our responses become more like:

That pencil snapping feels really frustrating.
Sometimes it feels like everything goes wrong.
Let's get you another one and make sure we pick a strong one! Then you will be able
    to get on with the work.

Changing how we respond, using compassion and offering containment, we enhance opportunities for connection. Remember that this is happening for us adults, too. Feeling rejected, needed, or not seen may trigger feelings of important previous relationships in which those feelings were substantial. At those times, our response can be in relation to the importance of that previous experience rather than proportionate to the current instance. If we hold that in mind and can recognise it is happening, the understanding can de-escalate our stress levels, help us be more compassionate, and increase the likelihood that what we do next will be helpful and provide emotional containment for ourselves and the other, maintaining the connection.

Being good enough

In 2019, *Science Daily* reported that 'good enough' parents probably only get it right about 50% of the time. That is enough for their children to develop secure attachments. Donald Winnicott (1974) introduced the phrase 'good enough' for the job of parenting. This idea could be extended to include any relational work in which we strive for a 'good enough way of being'. When we are building relationships with others, it won't be perfection, but our good intentions of wanting to understand and get it right some of the time is enough.

Perfect parenting is not, in fact, a perfect experience for the child (Tronick & Beeghly, 2011). The same is true of any para-attachment relationships, such as teacher–pupil relationships in school. We need early relationships to model the ups and downs of life. Repairing misattunements or less than ideal responses to needs and feelings is as important to our positive mental health as all the times we feel completely understood. Early experiences build our understanding of whether conflicts can be resolved, breaches in relationships can be repaired, and disconnections can be reconnected (Tronick & Beeghly, 2011; Lewis, 2000; Woolf, 2016). The belief that we can mend fractures in relationships leads to the development of trust and faith in ourselves and others; the fear that we cannot leads to mistrust and future difficulties with connection to others.

Connection

Relationships, rather than a seamless choreography, are always a work in progress. Working to more closely attune to another offers the reparative experience that builds resilience and trust in relationships. Broken bones can knit back stronger, just as fractured connections can strengthen through knowing the connection can be repaired. Building relationships in which discord is addressed and can be repaired is a therapeutic experience for those whose early relationships did not model this.

Therapeutic relationships in schools

Definitions for 'therapeutic' may talk of interventions which bring about better physical or mental health, as well as experiences which lead to relaxation or feelings of calm and happiness. In schools, we create environments where learning is facilitated. Feeling safe and, therefore, more relaxed is a therapeutic experience in education which supports better mental health and also allows the brain space for learning. Effective communication and a non-judgemental stance are important for developing therapeutic relationships (Rogers, 1995; Woolf, 2016). The therapeutic experience that a warm, compassionate, authentic relationship provides is evident across many of the helping professions, such as social care, health care, and education. Positive, therapeutic relationships can help to address early poor attachment relationships and experiences of loss, neglect, attack, and unpredictability.

Remedial relationships may play a part in reducing the impacts of adverse childhood experiences (ACEs) through the experience of feeling safe and cared for by consistent, trusted others (ACEsAware.org, n.d.). Supportive relationships with adults may make the difference between the child or young person experiencing chronic, damaging stress and experiencing stress as manageable (Bellis et al., 2017). Positive relationships provide therapeutic opportunities for containing emotions and making big feelings bearable. Through connection, the change from being overwhelmed or feeling stuck to managing and carrying on may provide for the feelings of being capable and courageous that are crucial to our sense of value and worth (Lew, 2002).

The term 'social buffering' describes the beneficial effects, both psychological and physiological, of social contact. While social environments are not always positive, the right social relationships boost the immune system, aid recovery from physical and mental injury, and are protective against mental illness (Kawachi & Berkman, 2001; Kikusui et al., 2006). Social buffering supports resilience and better mental health outcomes when it is available during challenging times (Sunderland, 2018). In early attachment relationships, part of the 'buffering' effect is through emotion regulation: adults supporting the young by holding and processing feelings for them first and then, as the child matures, working with them.

Throughout life, we use our interactions with others we feel safe with and connected to as sources of emotion regulation (Howe, 2011, Woolf, 2016). The stress buffering effects of parental relationships in early childhood continues until adolescence when the importance of parents in this role diminishes (Gunnar & Hostinar, 2015). By mid-childhood, friendships begin to be important as stress relievers (Gunnar & Hostinar, 2015). Peer-to-peer support is likely to emerge at a time when peers become more important generally (Blakemore, 2010; Erikson, 1995). Thoits (2011) described two forms of social support. The first type offers a safe, reliable relationship with someone who plays a helpful role in the life of the other, in our case a teacher. The second type of social support comes from peers, or those connected through similar experiences, who offer understanding and are an example of coping and how to go on (Thoits, 2011). Peer support may not always have the positive buffering impacts we would hope for (Veenstra & Laninga-Wijnen, 2022).

Social relationships and support are not always experienced without cost; if support is expected in return at times when we are emotionally depleted, this sense of responsibility for our support system can cause further stress. Sources of social buffering that are helpful when all goes well can, at other times, be sources of distress and feelings of social disconnection. Hostinar (2015) and Gunnar (2017) agree that both attachment relationships and peer relationships can offer social buffering from detrimental stress but that both can also be sources of stress themselves. Thoits (2011) suggested that having opportunities for both adult and peer elements of social support would offer a strong buffer to stress. Relationships in schools, both teacher with pupil and peer to peer, are important opportunities for creating healthy patterns of connecting with others. Teachers as sources of social support, along with having a sense of belonging in school, offer a social buffer which should not require a reciprocal level of support from the child or young person. This does not mean the pupil will not play their part in their group or deny that this gives them a sense of value and worth, but that their reserves are not drawn on to support others at a time when they are depleted.

Social support is a buffer, not a cure-all. Pupils live in communities where equality and fairness are not evident; where streets are not safe, housing is poor, and difference is stigmatised rather than celebrated. Economic stressors and differences in gender and age may cause differences in outcomes, even for those who do have social support networks (Kawachi & Berkman, 2001). Great schools and amazing teachers do not negate the realities of life or the deficiencies of society, and it is important that this is recognised and that we play our part in challenging inequity and exclusion in the demographics we serve (Ecclestone & Brunila, 2015). Despite external stressors, feeling you belong somewhere, that you have at least one adult there who offers support, and that the expectation of 'pay-back' there is only that you be yourself and that you are already 'enough' is a therapeutic experience likely to have a positive and long-lasting outcome.

Teachers' cognition of the role of social relationships in promoting physical, emotional, and social well-being informs the responsibility of educators for providing healthy environments where healthy relationships are fostered across the whole school population. The discussion around the role of schools and school staff in providing therapeutic environments and relationships is ongoing. Creating science-informed or evidence-based environments and relationships which promote learning and academic outcomes is a less controversial aim of education settings.

If we feel that it is our role to provide therapeutic experiences in schools, we may arrive at that from a deficit position – 'if not me then who' – or from a positive position in which we believe we are there to nurture and develop young minds in terms of knowledge and health and well-being. There are many reasons why we might believe it is our role to support the good mental health of our students. These include that we:

- believe education is about addressing the whole child
- can only teach children who are ready to learn when their emotional needs have been met

Connection

- are innately good at supporting student's emotional well-being
- see no one else is doing it.

Whatever our motivation, it is likely that pupils with attuned, caring, consistent teachers are more able to learn (De Thierry, 2015; Delaney, 2009). The more everyday relationships support relaxed feelings of being safe and valued, the more opportunities there are for recovery from adversities. Therapists working with CYP in schools recognise the value of education staff. While therapists can offer a skilled clinical intervention, parents and teachers who work together as a therapeutic team help the child or young person to develop better mental health (Beresford et al., 2018). Professor Sir Simon Wessely, lead on the 2018 review of the Mental Health Act (Department of Health and Social Care, 2018), agreed that the first line of support after traumatic experience is getting the right kind of support from everyday relationships.

Bridget Cooper (2004) described the culture in schools as having too much focus on too many areas in the curriculum, with standardisation and assessment at the core and individuality and personalised learning not prioritised. Through observation and interview, Cooper (2004) concluded that teachers do not feel valued. Asking more of our amazing school staff, who already do not have enough hours in the day for all they are already doing, could undoubtedly lead to feelings of alienation. There is a payoff for all when doing more to support better mental health in our classroom groups is about caring for both pupils and staff. If therapeutic schooling means that the academic tasks of the day can be more readily addressed, teacher stress may be reduced and increased time spent using therapeutic skills could reduce time spent addressing disruption in class. Emotional labour spent supporting pupils' mental well-being may diminish emotional labour needed for conflict resolution.

Therapeutic skills

Therapeutic skills, based on counselling skills, are interpersonal skills which can be effectively employed by warm, empathic helping professionals. Therapeutic skills are sometimes called helping skills. Helping in this sense does not mean 'doing to', or 'doing for' but, rather, 'being with'. 'Therapeutic' can be perceived as disempowering or creating a sense of vulnerability, and some definitions can support this idea. Therapeutic relationships in school are not about 'causing' better mental health but, rather, offering warm, consistent connections that support pupils' holistic development. Therapeutic ways of being, like offering compassion for everyone and containment at times of overwhelm, are about building positive beliefs about the world and the self which support connection as well as supporting the pupil's own skills for self-regulation and independence.

Therapeutic skills include:

- being able to both be available and supportive in listening, especially when the narrative of the speaker is hard to tell and hard to hear
- being able to be with the other while allowing and supporting them in finding their own solutions
- being able to support others in reflecting on their ways of being and whether new ways of relating or responding could be more helpful

- being able to support autonomy and self-determination rather than promote dependence and reliance on others (Columbus, 2021; Westergaard, 2017; Woolf, 2016).

There are arguments against therapeutic education (Ecclestone & Hayes, 2009; Furedi, 2004; Wright, 2014) that we need to bear in mind. Amongst Ecclestone's (2011) concerns is the idea that we are in danger of making students see themselves as vulnerable or fragile. The potential 'dangers', or risks, of a therapeutic ethos include:

- power dynamics – the teacher has power over a disempowered child
- increasing vulnerability – children being made to see themselves as fragile, damaged, and needy.

For me, if what we do is having this effect, then this is not a therapeutic approach. My belief about ways to offer a therapeutic approach in school is that we model:

- I believe in you.
- I believe you can find a solution/sort a problem.
- I am here.
- I will keep you safe.
- I care about you but do not believe you always need me or my protection, but I am here if you do.
- I am interested in you and your experiences and feelings, but I only need to know what you choose to tell me.
- I know people grow through adversity and most are not destroyed by it.

An argument against therapeutic culture in education which is harder to counter is that we pathologise social ills and then address the resulting psychological symptoms when we are unable to address social inequalities such as poverty and social exclusion (Ecclestone & Brunila, 2015). Changes in school policies and practices are important ways we can stop perpetuating social inequality, but education settings alone are not able to address the root causes of social injustice (Nalani et al., 2021). Medical professionals share the ethical disquiet about treating issues arising from social injustices through medical interventions; again, the medical intervention is helpful, but the efficacy is hindered when other social root causes of ill health are not also being addressed (Andermann & CLEAR Collaboration, 2016). The role of education should not be to meet pupils' basic needs, such as food and shelter, but, rather, to meet the cognitive desires to know and to understand and to prepare pupils to achieve fulfilling lives. Focussing on student emotional needs may substitute for addressing wider social ills; this can give messages to students that we are not in connection with their reality.

There are points that are important to consider when including therapeutic approaches in our teaching toolbox. We may agree with Ecclestone and Brunila's (2015) wider advocacy for social justice as a key to improving the mental health of CYP. To many of us, it will be clear that better housing, safer housing estates, easier access to opportunities through accessible public transport and leisure activities, more social care support, and more sensitive policing and equality in access to the justice system would be life changing. It can feel frustrating to be the service that supports the child's resilience and drive to be and do well, in spite of things outside the immediate influence and control of school staff.

Connection

Relationships and environments in school matter, whatever the pupil's experiences of people and places are outside the school gates. Education and schooling are recognised as a route out of many of the 'social ills' referred to by Ecclestone and Brunila (2015). A 2019 paper from the European Commission illustrated the benefits of education and skills across many areas. Their findings were that benefits included a higher likelihood of employment, higher income, more engagement in cultural activities and in further education, and better health and well-being.

Good attendance at school results in better health, education, and socioeconomic outcomes (Public Health England, 2021). Public Health England (2021) identified that the pupils who attend and attain at school are often those with good physical and emotional health and that the children who thrive at school are then better placed to act on information about good health throughout life. Schools support children doing well when their lives outside of school also support this. Schools may offer relationships and environments for change for those CYP who do not have such strong starting points. Creating classrooms and schools where pupils want to be is important to lifelong chances for financial health as well as physical, emotional, and social health. Wanting to be in school can be about a feeling of connection to the school community, be that a strong positive relationship with one or more members of staff or a feeling of belonging within the peer group.

A sense of belonging in school

A sense of belonging is a solid foundation, a type of secure base, from which we explore and make sense of our world and create meaning in our lives. In early life, our sense of belonging is to a small group, often close family, that expands as we grow and as our brains develop. Family, friends, community, and our world opens up, and our sense of belonging, or of alienation, can become more flexible and open to growth or more rigid and less adaptable to change. For some, the sense of belonging to a tribe, a social group with one or more areas of commonality, can be through a shared identity, experience, or demographic. Connection to nature, spiritual dimensions, or place and time can also provide a sense of belonging.

Having a sense of belonging, 'fitting in' and relating to a group, is directly linked to people finding life meaningful (Lambert et al., 2013). This is important for mental health as, increasingly, we understand good mental health is not measured by happiness but, rather, by a sense of fulfilment or of meaning. In Wales, belonging has been recognised in the new curriculum (Welsh Government, 2020) as a valued experience in the nation and in the cultural community.

How often do we think about whether we create a sense of belonging in school? School connectedness or school bonding are other terms used in research on the value of feelings of belonging in schools. A sense of belonging in school has positive impacts on attendance and engagement during schooling and long-term benefits for emotional well-being and academic, financial, and employment outcomes (Abdollahi & Noltemeyer, 2018; Allen et al., 2021; Cozolino, 2014; Jennings & Greenberg, 2009; Korpershoek et al., 2020; NFER, 2021). A sense of school belonging may decrease risks for both physical and mental health; feeling 'disconnected' is more likely to link to truancy as well as other behaviours that lead to detrimental physical and social outcomes (Thomas & Smith, 2004). These are likely to have subsequent negative impacts on life chances. As such, school belongingness warrants our interest and attention.

Nearly 80 years ago, Abraham Maslow (1943) recognised the importance of a sense of belonging in his 'hierarchy of needs'. Erik Erikson (1995), 20 years later, described his stages of psychosocial development, with the importance in adolescence of finding the group in which they belong and build meaningful relationships. The strength of personal relationships and a sense of belonging are key for 15-year-olds, as those of this age who have a strong sense of belonging at school report having the most satisfaction with life (National Foundation for Educational Research, 2021). Both Maslow's and Erikson's models of developmental needs demonstrate that, once basic physical and emotional needs are met, and we pass the stage of dependency on family and carers, belonging to a group outside of the home builds our sense of identity and purpose in life. Relationships during adolescence can be challenging; not feeling so grounded in family, while experiencing peer relationships as fluctuating and unpredictable, can mean that, during the teenage years, a lot of energy and attention has to be used in order to gain stability and identity through belonging to a group (Allen et al., 2021). Most of us remember the exhilaration and fear of our independence from family and our dependence on friendships at this stage of our life. A sense of belonging or connectedness to school can be cultivated and nurtured, meaning this is one of the areas we can address in order to develop better mental health in schools.

Developing a sense of belonging

Kindness and kinship both contain the Old English root 'kin', meaning family or sort (Ballat et al., 2020; Campling, 2013). Kindness to others can build kinship: feelings of being connected and of the 'same sort'. Connection or belonging to the group makes kindness between members more likely. When we share experiences, rituals, struggles, and goals, it engenders a sense of investment in the group. In schools, we can create that sense of kinship, being 'of a kind', through a variety of elements during the life of the school.

Create special traditions for your class

Traditions can help create positive feelings and build shared commitments to the group. Having traditions, shared unique verbal or non-verbal language, and other elements common and exclusive to the group, can develop the group, class, or school into a tribe. Feeling included leads to feelings of protection and acceptance, which are innate needs throughout life. Familiar processes and procedures create a sense of security (Jennings & Greenberg, 2009).

Be a person as well as a teacher

One report from Canada suggested that teachers can foster a sense of belonging by offering personal as well as academic support to students (St-Amand et al., 2017). Pupils who see their teacher as a person as well as an educator may feel more included in the teacher's tribe. Teacher support and positive personal characteristics were the strongest predictors of school belonging for pupils during adolescence (Wigford & Higgins, 2019). The importance of teacher warmth and support in creating a sense of belonging contrasts with the detrimental effects of critical and belittling teachers who foster

Connection

feelings of alienation and disconnection that are particularly damaging in adolescent years (Riley, 2019; Shaw, 2019; Wigford & Higgins, 2019).

Offer enduring relationships

There are particular benefits for pupils who feel that support from their teacher is always available to them (Bellis et al., 2017). The sense that we can create a relationship that lasts over time, and of ongoing care and support, may be most helpful in combating the development of poor mental health. Relationships that offer frequent positive contact over long periods of time are ideal for creating feelings of belonging (Over, 2016). The value of positive interactions is clear, but it is worth reflecting on how we offer frequent interactions that continue and endure. Year tutors in secondary schools who follow the year group throughout the school is one example. Form teachers who welcome ex-pupils to interact with them once they have moved on in the school is another. Subject teachers or specialist staff may offer this to classes or groups during each year in their schooling. Exploration of practical and realistic ways to offer enduring relationships in secondary education settings is important, as this is a developmental stage in which pupils may benefit most from feelings of belonging in their school community.

Offer a variety of activities which encourage working in groups or teams

'Team building' is so commonly referred to that we may not have considered its benefits. Consistently working on team or group problem-solving is the very basis of human survival. No wonder solving problems, creating solutions, and making life better in collaboration with others makes us feel so good. The feel-good satisfaction of a job well done leaves us with a sense of belonging to a group. Struggling and persevering, even without a successful outcome, can also draw us together with our tribe. Joint enterprise through play and playful activities is not only a powerful team building experience but also is shown to offer conditions for relational repair (Kemp et al., 2016) to which we can return to the feeling of being part of our tribe. Joint activities such as music and movement build group feeling. Moving in time with each other, sharing a rhythm or beat, makes people feel more positively about each other (Tunçgenç & Cohen, 2016), and singing together promotes social bonds and swiftly builds new relationships (Pearce et al., 2015). Playful and physical collaborations help to engender group bonding.

Allow for and recognise the value of play

The human need for connection requires a medium in which connections are built. Play is one of the most powerful media for creating, maintaining, and deepening connection (Woolf, 2016). One of the main reasons the young of many species engage in play is as a way of connecting (Bekoff, 2001; Cohen, 2001). Play supports the development of early attachment relationships (Mears, 2005; Winnicott, 1974) and helps us to manage separation from and maturation away from attachment figures (Panksepp, in Weintraub, 2012). Players are equal in a play world despite their difference in status in the real world. In early years, play reciprocity is already important for social friendships and social inclusion (Coelho et al., 2017). Children prefer connecting with playful children. Playfulness is a muscle that benefits from lots of use, and the more that groups play together, the more they want to stay together.

Play is not only important in building and maintaining social relationships but can also be a powerful medium for overcoming difference and promoting inclusion (Antonacci et al., 2010). Play provides groups with a collective purpose which creates group cohesion (Henricks, 2015) and a sense of belonging for all, including newcomers. When meeting new people, engaging in play can enhance the development of feelings of friendship and can facilitate the change from stranger to friend (Antonacci et al., 2010). In already established relationships, play offers a medium of repair, a time to reconnect if connection has been challenged or broken (Cohen, 2001; Kemp et al., 2016). It is likely that the cohesion of a group will require frequent opportunities for re-establishing and refreshing old relationships while integrating new ones (Antonacci et al., 2010). Play has value for each individual player, as better social and mental health in individuals increases social cohesion between individuals. The benefits of play for self and for connection to others supports social and emotional well-being in the wider communities around our schools (Woolf, 2016). Communities in which pupils have a sense of belonging in their school will, over time, have more and more members who have a mutual feeling of connection to the local school and, therefore, one point of similarity, or kinship, with each other.

Creating change for a sense of belonging

The 2017 Programme for International Student Assessment (PISA) published a report: 'Students' sense of belonging at school and their relations with teachers'. It found that the sense of belonging was not as strong now as in previous years. Reflecting on this and understanding the causes of this change could help us to find the remedy. It was also clear to the report authors that disadvantaged students were less likely to feel that they belong than their more advantaged peers. Evidence suggested that students who felt like 'outsiders' did not do as well in their work.

Reflecting in 2020 about 'Place and Belonging in Schools: Why it Matters Today', Riley et al. concluded that implementing a policy that prioritises the aim of fostering belonging in schools would require a major change of direction from the government in England. The authors advocated that the government shift from a focus on accountability and targets for results to aspirations to create schools where young people are supported to feel fulfilled and to find their own way to contribute to society. In 2018, Riley et al. identified that the environment, relationships, and feelings of having influence and being effective all feed into a sense of belonging. Others, such as Bucholz and Sheffler (2009), found that the relevance of the curriculum to student groups is as important as relationships with staff and peers for a sense of belonging. They still advocated, though, for the role of the good listener in making students feel that they are valued members of their school community. Listening with compassion and genuine interest helps CYP to feel that they have truly been heard, and the listener has genuinely attempted to 'feel' their communicated experience (Murdoch et al., 2020; Siegel, 1999). Feeling valued, through experiencing interest and attention from teachers, enhances self-esteem and a sense of being a significant member of the group. Cozolino (2014) saw schools or classrooms as 'tribes' – a secure base where we feel safe. Through such relationships, we learn about ourselves (Winnicott, 1974). The desire to be a part of a group offers opportunities for experiencing that we can play our part, which builds feelings of value and self-worth.

Paying more attention to creating feelings of belonging in schools, particularly in class groups, could increase the satisfaction of pupils with their places of learning.

Connection

Feeling connected to peers in the classroom, that fairness is upheld, and that they have a role in maintaining the well-being of the group can be further developed through extra-curricular activities outside the classroom (Thomas & Smith, 2004). Thomas and Smith (2004) found that smaller schools are more likely to foster feelings of school belonging-ness. Jennings and Greenberg (2009) suggested that secondary schools may have more need to develop school connectedness. Although they do not refer to school size as a reason why high schools are singled out as in need of additional consideration, it is hard not to see how if 'size matters', and secondary schools are often markedly larger than primary settings, this is an issue that can impact outcomes.

Evidence suggests a sense of belonging in school could also address targets currently seen as the core measurement of school performance, such as attendance and academic results. Belongingness leads to less absenteeism, more likelihood of remaining in school post-compulsory education, and some increase in academic achievement (Korpershoek et al., 2020). Not feeling affiliated to school may mean less incentive to attend or to remain once able to leave. In this increasingly fragmented society, where online groups mean more to many than being with others in the physical world, the win-win of devel-oping a sense of belonging in schools can support the positive mental health of pupils as well as their educational outcomes.

Conclusion

Connection is a core human need. While attachment theory tells us that early caretak-ing relationships are the foundation for later relationships throughout life, those later relationships can change patterns in the ways that we connect with others. Teachers are amongst the main influences in our lives in the larger world. Teachers may be very different from other adults that children are familiar with. Children have to create a new map of this new relationship. We in school help to form the new pathways of how the world-away-from-home works. For some children, connection to others is the reward for school tasks rather than classroom approvals such as stickers, points, or praise (Knight, 2021). This therapeutic experience of positive connection means more than points or prizes.

If we give children a solid floor to stand on, they may find that giving up or getting out are not always necessary strategies. When we consistently and respectfully offer a helping hand out of those tricky places in which we all sometimes find ourselves, we may model that some people offer genuine support with no strings attached and no hidden agenda. If we agree that a child's basic need for a secure base, support with emotion regulation, and a sense of being among kin have to be met before academic learning can occur (BPS, 2020; Knight, 2018), we acknowledge the importance of connections in schools. When we are informed and aware of the knowledge we need, teachers can make informed decisions about the kind of educator they want to be and believe is in the best interests of students. This, of course, is within the constraints of our contracts, whole school approach, government guidance, and parent expectations, which is a discussion at the heart of this book. You cannot legislate for whether or not schools provide therapeutic environments or whether teachers offer therapeutic relationships. Some teachers leave you feeling better, calmer, more accepted, and understood just because that is how and who they are. Compassionate, containing others who understand us and to whom we feel connected are a balm for the soul, and energise us to be better, do better, and be that person for other people in our world.

92

> **REFLECTION TASK 4: BALANCING THERAPEUTIC AND TEACHING RELATIONSHIPS**
>
> Therapeutic relationships must strike a balance:
>
> - Why, how, and when do I help students?
> - Why and when do I 'stay with' students struggles and challenges, believing they can manage?
>
> Self-awareness is a skill that enhances the likelihood we offer relationships that support growth and do not diminish the other.
>
> - Do I need or enjoy being helpful and, therefore, do not recognise when over-helpfulness is intrusive or denies the child autonomy?
> - Do I dislike the feeling of being needed or relied upon and, therefore, do not recognise when I am dismissive or do not respond to needs of students?
>
> What does 'belonging' mean to you?
>
> - When you feel you don't belong, what does that feel like?
> - Why might it be important for a student to have a sense of belonging?
> - What were your own experiences of a sense of belonging in school/ college?
> - What impact has that had on your sense of self as a learner?

References

Abdollahi, A. and Noltemeyer, A. (2018) Academic hardiness: Mediator between sense of belonging to school and academic achievement? *Journal of Educational Research*, 111(3), 345–351.

ACEsAware.org (n.d.) Clinical response to ACEs and toxic stress. Available from: https://www .acesaware.org/wp-content/uploads/2020/05/Provider-Toolkit-Clinical-Response-to-ACEs -and-Toxic-Stress.pdf [Accessed 24th December 2021].

Allen, K-A., Gray, D., Baumeister, R. and Leary, M. (2021) The need to belong: A deep dive into the origins, implications, and future of a foundational construct. *Educational Psychology Review*, Aug, 31, 1–24.

Andermann, A. and CLEAR Collaboration (2016) Taking action on the social determinants of health in clinical practice: A framework for health professionals. *Canadian Medical Association Journal*, 188, 17–18.

Antonacci, D., Norscia, I. and Palagi, E. (2010) Stranger to familiar: Wild strepsirhines manage xenophobia by playing. *PLoS ONE*, 5(10). Available from: https://journals.plos.org/plosone/ article?id=10.1371/journal.pone.0013218. [Accessed 04th March 2020].

Ballatt, J., Campling, P. and Maloney, C. (2020) *Intelligent Kindness: Rehabilitating the Welfare State*. 2nd ed. Cambridge: Cambridge University Press.

Baumeister, R. and Robson, D. (2021) Belongingness and the modern schoolchild: On loneliness, socioemotional health, self-esteem, evolutionary mismatch, online sociality, and the numbness of rejection. *Australian Journal of Psychology*, 73 (1), 103–111.

Connection

Bekoff (2001) Social play, behaviour, cooperation, fairness, trust, band the evolution of morality, *Journal of Consciousness Studies*, 8 (2), 81–90.

Bellis, M., Hardcastle, K., Ford, K., Hughes, K., Ashton, K., Quigg, Z. and Butler, N. (2017) Does continuous trusted adult support in childhood impart life-course resilience against adverse childhood experiences: A retrospective study on adult health-harming behaviours and mental well-being. *BMC Psychiatry,* 17 (110). Available from: doi: 10.1186/s12888-017-1305-3

Beresford, B., Clarke, S. and Maddison, J. (2018) Therapy interventions for children with neurodisabilities: A qualitative scoping study. *Health Technology Assessment*, 22 (3), 1–150.

Berkman, L. (1995) The role of social relations in health promotion. *Psychosomatic Medecine* 57, 245–254.

Blakemore, S-J, (2010) The developing social brain: Implications for education. *Neuron*, 65 (6), 744–747.

British Psychological Society (BPS) (2020) *Emotionally Regulate Before We Educate: Focusing on Psychological Wellbeing in the Approach to a New School Day.* Leicester: BPS.

Bowlby, J. (1973) *Attachment and Loss: Vol. 2. Separation.* New York: Basic Books.

Bowlby, J. (1982) Attachment and loss: Retrospect and prospect. *American Journal of Orthopsychiatry*, 52 (4), 664–678.

Bucholz, J. and Sheffler, J. (2009) Creating a warm and inclusive classroom environment: Planning for all children to feel welcome. *Electronic Journal for Inclusive Education*, 2 (4). Available from: https://corescholar.libraries.wright.edu/cgi/viewcontent.cgi?article=1102&context=ejie. [Accessed 14th December 2021].

Campling, P. (2013) Culture, kinship and intelligent kindness. Available from: https://www.rcpsych.ac.uk/docs/default-source/members/sigs/spirituality-spsig/spirituality-special-interest-group-publications-penny-campling-culture-kinship-and-intelligent-kindness.pdf?sfvrsn=45f6fb33_2 [Accessed 15th December 2021].

Coelho, L., Torres, N., Carla Fernandes, C. and Santos, A. (2017) Quality of play, social acceptance and reciprocal friendship in preschool children. *European Early Childhood Education Research Journal*, 25 (6), 812–823.

Cohen, L. (2001) *Playful Parenting.* New York: Ballantine Books.

Columbus, K. (2021) *How to Listen: Tools for Opening up Conversations When it Matters Most.* London: Kyle Books.

Cooper, B. (2004) Empathy, interaction and caring: Teachers' roles in a constrained environment. *Pastoral Care in Education*, 22 (3), 12–21.

Cozolino, L. (2014) *Attachment-Based Teaching. Creating a Tribal Classroom.* New York: Norton and Co.

De Thierry, B. (2015) *Teaching the Child on the Trauma Continuum.* Guilford: Grosvenor House Publishing

Delaney, M. (2009) *Teaching the Unteachable.* London: Worth Publishing.

Department of Health and Social Care (DfHSC) (2018) Modernising the mental health act: Final report from the independent review. Available from: https://www.gov.uk/government/publications/modernising-the-mental-health-act-final-report-from-the-independent-review [Accessed 29th July 2021].

Di Nicola, V. (2019) "A person is a person through other persons": A social psychiatry manifesto for the 21st century. *World Social Psychiatry*, 1, 8–21.

Ecclestone, K. (2011) Emotionally-vulnerable subjects and new inequalities: The educational implications of a new 'epistemology of the emotions'. *International Journal of Sociology of Education*, 21 (2), 91–113.

Ecclestone, K. and Brunila, K. (2015) Governing emotionally vulnerable subjects and 'therapisation' of social justice. *Pedagogy, Culture and Society*, 23 (4), 485–506.

Ecclestone, K. and Hayes, D. (2009) *The Dangerous Rise of Therapeutic Education.* Abingdon: Routledge.

Erikson, E. (1995) *Play and Society.* London: Vintage.

European Commission (2019) *Impact of Education and Skills on Life Chances.* Luxembourg: European Commission.

Ford, J., Anderson, C., Gillespie, S., Giurgescu, C., Nolan, T., Nowak, A. and Williams, K. (2019) Social integration and quality of social relationships as protective factors for inflammation in a nationally representative sample of black women. *Journal of Urban Health*, 96 (Suppl 1), S35–S43.

Furedi, F. (2004) *Therapy Culture: Creating Vulnerability in an Uncertain Age.* London: Routledge.

Gerber, Z. & Anaki, D. (2021) The role of self-compassion, concern for others, and basic psychological needs in the reduction of caregiving burnout. *Mindfulness,* 12, 741–750.

Gunnar, M. (2017) Social buffering of stress in development: A career perspective. *Perspectives on Psychological Science*, 12 (3), 355–373.

Gunnar, M. and Hostinar, C. (2015) The social buffering of the hypothalamic-pituitary-adrenocortical axis in humans: Developmental and experiential determinants. *Social Neuroscience*, 10 (5), 479–488.

Henricks (2015) *Play and the Human Condition.* Champaign: University of Illinois Press.

Holt-Lunstad J. (2021) The major health implications of social connection. *Current Directions in Psychological Science*, 30 (3), 251–259.

Holt-Lunstad, J., Smith T. and Layton, J. (2010) Social relationships and mortality risk: A meta-analytic review. *PLOS Medicine*, 7 (7) (online) Available from: doi: 10.1371/journal.pmed .1000316

Hostinar, C. (2015) Recent Developments in the Study of Social Relationships, Stress Responses, and Physical Health. *Current Opinion in Psychology*, May, 1 (5), 90–95.

Howe, D. (2011) *Attachment Across the Life Course: A Brief Introduction.* Basingstoke: Palgrave Macmillan.

Jennings, P. and Greenberg M. (2009) The prosocial classroom: Teacher social and emotional competence in relation to student and classroom outcomes. *Review of Educational Research*, 79 (1), 491–525.

Kawachi, I. and Berkman, L. (2001) Social ties and mental health. *Journal of Urban Health*, Sep, 78 (3), 458–467.

Kemp, C., Lunkenheimer, E., Albrecht, E. and Deborah Chen, D. (2016) Can we fix this? Parent–Child repair processes and preschoolers' regulatory skills. *Family Relations*, October, 65 (4), 576–590.

Kikusui, T, Winslow, J. and Mori, Y. (2006) Social buffering: Relief from stress and anxiety. *Philosophical Transactions of the Royal Society B, Biological Sciiences*, Dec 29, 361 (1476), 2215–2228.

Klein, J. (1987) *Our Need for Others and its Roots in Infancy* London: Routledge.

Knight, S. (2018) The therapeutic teacher. *Headteacher Update.* Available from: http://www .headteacher-update.com/best-practice-article/the-therapeutic-teacher/195018/. [Accessed 26th September 2021].

Knight, S. (2021) The dos and don'ts of attachment behaviours. *Headteacher Update, Best Practice Focus*, 06 September. Available from: https://www.headteacher-update.com/knowledge-bank /trauma-and-insecure-attachment-behaviour-in-primary-schools-how-to-respond-primary -schools-therapeutic-practice-classroom-management-teaching-learning-sanctions-detention -exclusion-inclusion/240540/ [Accessed 14th October 2021].

Korpershoek, H., Canrinus,E., Fokkens-Bruinsma, M. and de Boer, H. (2020) The relationships between school belonging and students' motivational, social-emotional, behavioural, and academic outcomes in secondary education: A meta-analytic review. *Research Papers in Education*, 35 (6), 641–680.

Lambert, N., Stillman T., Hicks J., Kamble S., Baumeister R. and Fincham F. (2013) To belong is to matter: Sense of belonging enhances meaning in life. *Personality and Social Psychology Bulletin*, 39 (11), 1418–1427.

Lew, A. (2002) Helping children cope in an increasingly threatening world: Four cornerstones of emotional well-being. *The Family Journal: Counseling and Therapy for Couples and Families*, April, 10 (2), 134–138.

Lewis, J. (2000) Repairing the bond in important relationships: A dynamic for personality maturation. *Americal Journal of Psychiatry*, 157, 1375–1378.

Lieberman, M. (2015) *Social: Why Our Brains Are Wired to Connect*. Oxford: Oxford University Press.

Maslow, A. (1943) A theory of human motivation. *Psychological Review*, 50 (4), 430–437.

McCrory, E. (2021) Transformation Seminar: Childhood trauma and the brain: What have we learnt from neuroscience? March 10. Available from: https://www.youtube.com/watch?v=uj-8D7L-coE. [Accessed 13th April 2021].

Mears, R. (2005) *The Metaphor of Play: Origin and Breakdown of Personal Being*. London: Routledge.

Murdoch, D., English, A., Hintz, A. and Tyson, K. (2020) Feeling heard: Inclusive education, transformative learning, and productive struggle. *Educational Theory*, 70, 653–679.

Nalani, A., Yoshikawa, H. and Carter, P. (2021) Social science–based pathways to reduce social inequality in youth outcomes and opportunities at scale. *Socius: Sociological Research for a Dynamic World*, 7, 1–17.

National Foundation for Educational Research in England and Wales (NFER) (2021) NFER analysis of wellbeing of 15-year-olds reveals strength of personal relationships and a sense of belonging key. Available from: https://www.nfer.ac.uk/news-events/press-releases/nfer-analysis-of-wellbeing-of-15-year-olds-reveals-strength-of-personal-relationships-and-a-sense-of-belonging-key/ [Accessed 26th November 2021].

Over, H. (2016) The origins of belonging: Social motivation in infants and young children. *PhilosophicalTransactions of the Royal Society, Biological Sciences* 371 (1686) 20150072. Available from: doi.org/10.1098/rstb.2015.0072

Pearce, E., Launay, J. and Dunbar, R. (2015) The ice-breaker effect: Singing mediates fast social bonding. *Royal Society Open Science.*, October, 2 (10) 150221. Available from: doi.org/10.1098/rsos.150221

Pittman, L. and Richmond, A. (2007) Academic and psychological functioning in late adolescence: The importance of school belonging. *The Journal of Experimental Education*, 75 (4), 270–290.

Porges, S. (2009) The polyvagal theory: New insights into adaptive reactions of the autonomic nervous system. *Cleveland Clinical Journal of Medicine*, 76 (Supplement 2), S86–S90.

Programme for International Student Assessment (PISA) (2017) Students' sense of belonging at school and their relations with teachers. Available from: https://www.oecd.org/education/pisa-2015-results-volume-iii-9789264273856-en.htm [Accessed 12th November 2021].

Public Health England (2021) School-aged years high impact area 4: Reducing vulnerabilities and improving life chances. May 19. Available from: https://www.gov.uk/government/publications/commissioning-of-public-health-services-for-children/school-aged-years-high-impact-area-4-reducing-vulnerabilities-and-improving-life-chances [Accessed 17th December 2021].

Riley, K. (2019) Agency and belonging: What transformative actions can schools take to help create a sense of place and belonging? In British Psychological Society (BPS) Creating a culture of belonging in a school context. *Educational & Child Psychology*, 36 (4), 91–103.

Riley, K., Coates, M. and Martinez, S. (2018) Place and belonging in schools: Unlocking possibilities. Available from: www.ucl.ac.uk/ioe-place-and-belonging-in-schools [Accessed 19th January 2022].

Riley, K., Coates, M. and Allen, T. (2020) Place and belonging in schools: Why it matters today. Available from: https://neu.org.uk/media/13026/view [Accessed 19th January 2022].

Rogers, C. (1995) *On Becoming a Person: A Therapist's View of Psychotherapy*. 2nd ed. Boston: Houghton Mifflin.

Science Daily (2019) 'Good enough' parenting is good enough, study finds. May 08 Available from: https://www.sciencedaily.com/releases/2019/05/190508134511.htm [Accessed 23rd September 2021].

Shaw, E. (2019) 'How do I know that I belong?' Exploring secondary aged pupils' views on what it means to belong to their school. In British Psychological Society (BPS) Creating a culture of belonging in a school context. *Educational & Child Psychology*, December, 36 (4), 79–91.

Siegel, D. (1999) *The Developing Mind: How Relationships and the Brain Interact to Shape Who We Are*. New York: Guilford Press.

Smith, T. and Weihs, K. (2019) Emotion, social relationships, and physical health: Concepts, methods, and evidence for an integrative perspective. *Psychosomatic Medicine*, October, 81 (8), 681–693.

Sorel E. (2019) The social brain: Wired to connect and belong. *World Social Psychiatry*, 1 (1), 23–24.

St-Amand, J., Girard, S. and Smith J. (2017) Sense of belonging at school: Defining attributes, determinants, and sustaining strategies. *IAFOR Journal of Education*, 5 (2), 105–119.

Sunderland, M. (2016) *The Science of Parenting*. 2nd ed. London: DK Publishing.

Sunderland, M. (2018) Mental health: Spotting and averting issues in schools. *SecEd Online Magazine*. Available from: https://www.sec-ed.co.uk/best-practice/mental-health-spotting-and-averting-issues-in-schools/ [Accessed 22nd December 2021].

Thoits, P. (2011) Mechanisms linking social ties and support to physical and mental health. *Journal of Health and Social Behavior*, 52 (2), 145–161.

Thomas, S. and Smith, H. (2004) School connectedness, anger behaviors, and relationships of violent and nonviolent American youth. *Perspectives in Psychiatric Care*, 40, 135–148.

Tronick, E. and Beeghly, M. (2011) Infants' meaning-making and the development of mental health problems. *Am Psychol*, 66 (2), 107–119.

Tunçgenç, B. and Cohen, E. (2016) Movement synchrony forges social bonds across group divides. *Frontiers in Psychology*, 7, 782. Available from: doi: 10.3389/fpsyg.2016.00782

Umberson, D. and Montez, J. (2010) Social relationships and health: A flashpoint for health policy. *Journal of Health and Social Behavior*, 51 (Suppl), S54–S66.

Veenstra, R. and Laninga-Wijnen, L. (2022) Peer network studies and interventions in adolescence. *Current Opinion in Psychology*, 44, 157–163.

Weintraub, P. (2012) Discover interview: Jaak Panksepp pinned down humanity's 7 primal emotions. *Discover* May 31, 1:00 AM Available from: https://www.discovermagazine.com/mind/discover-interview-jaak-panksepp-pinned-down-humanitys-7-primal-emotions [Accessed 19th October 2021].

Welsh Government (2020) Curriculum for Wales guidance. Available from: https://hwb.gov.wales/storage/b44ad45b-ff78-430a-9423-36feb86aaf7e/curriculum-for-wales-guidance.pdf [Accessed 01st January 2022].

Westergaard, J. (2017) *An Introduction to Helping Skills: Counselling, Coaching and Mentoring*. London: Sage Publications.

Wigford, A. and Higgins, A. (2019) Wellbeing in international schools: Teachers' perceptions. In British Psychological Society (BPS) Creating a culture of belonging in a school context. *Educational & Child Psychology*, December, 36 (4), 46–64.

Winnicott, D. (1974) *Playing and Reality*. Middlesex: Pelican Books.

Woolf, A. (2016) *Better Play: Practical Strategies for Supporting Play in Schools for Children of all Ages*. Driffield: Worth Publishing

Wright, K. (2014) Student wellbeing and the therapeutic turn in education. *The Australian Educational and Developmental Psychologist Directions*, 31 (2), 141–152.

Chapter 6

What are schools for?

What is the point of education?

Education should be designed and implemented to equip pupils for their future and the future of their communities and of the wider world. Education must not rely on the doctrine of the past; however, it should not lose sight of the pure enjoyment of learning for learning's sake, and the importance of being grounded in, and informed by, the historical attainments and failures of the community's cultural past. Whatever education provision offers, it is about preparing learners for their futures in a world they will both respond to and shape.

It is possible that, despite choosing a career in education and passionately giving our energy, commitment, and creativity to educating those in our charge, we have not often questioned the purpose of our quest. Rethinking education (BBC, 2021a) means addressing the question, 'what is education for?' Whether policy-makers believe it is for the benefit of the person being educated or for the benefit of the state providing the education, their ideology directs the nature of the education being provided. The connection between the purpose of schools and mental health is two-fold:

- does the purpose of education include a responsibility for building good mental health?
- does the purpose of education not include responsibility for mental well-being; at the same time, does education's responsibility for academic success lead to negative impacts on mental health?

Knowing the purpose of education in the UK matters because it could indicate that providing for better mental health through school provisions is an explicit or implicit part of our professional responsibilities. It matters because if we knew that providing provisions for better mental health in schools was not a part of our professional role, we would know that we are not required (and are not resourced) to address mental health needs in our pupils. If the purpose of our role may have an unintended consequence that pupils' mental health can be negatively impacted, we may feel that the remedy for this lies outside of schools with other services and that communities must 'step up' to resolve this.

DOI: 10.4324/9781003277903-7

What are schools for?

Those invested in the provision and delivery of education cite a variety of aims:

- to safeguard knowledge (Scruton, 2016)
- to facilitate social progress (Smith, 2018)
- to drive economic growth (DfE, 2021)
- to develop all the talents, skills, and abilities of pupils (Department of Education (NI), n.d.).

Each of these aims could be a sole rationale for education settings or the principal objective for provisions in schools. They may combine together to inform the school environment, relationships, and curriculum provision.

Sir Ken Robinson (2017) described an aim for contemporary education that fits with what is needed now and allows for what may be needed in the future. He felt that the purpose of education was to give every pupil the opportunity to learn about both their internal and external world. Knowing and understanding ourselves and others, comprehending the way relationships work between the two, and having knowledge and understanding of the world we live in prepares pupils for future lives well lived.

Pupils should leave education:

- having knowledge about the world around them
- possessing a wide understanding of cultures and histories
- being able to engage with the world in ways that economically benefit both individuals and the community
- being integrated into cultural and community activity
- having positive relationships with close and wider groups that foster a sense of belonging
- having a sense of purpose, meaning, and personal fulfilment in living a congruent, authentic life.

Safeguarding knowledge for individual and collective benefit

In 2021, Nick Gibb, then Minister of State at the Department for Education in England, gave a speech on raising school standards. His vision of education in England was that 'we are the true romantics – believing in education for education's sake'. He advocated for the importance of a knowledge-rich curriculum in which schools give every child access to 'the knowledge they are entitled to as part of their cultural inheritance' (Gibb, 2021). Gibb (2021) saw the outcome of delivering a knowledge-rich curriculum as positive for individuals in terms of their well-being, essential for social equality, and for equipping pupils for life in the twenty-first century, although the mechanism of how one leads to the other was not explained. Gibb believed that the more shared knowledge we have as a society, the more integrated and inclusive that society; however, this seemed wedded to a narrow view in which delivering shared knowledge can only happen if schools teach a knowledge-based rather than competence-based curriculum (Gibb, 2021).

Not everyone agrees with this view; many feel that in order to be 'future-ready', developing competencies is more helpful than delivering knowledge (Bellanca & Brandt, 2010; Stehle & Peters-Burton, 2019; Tan et al., 2017). There may be no universal definition of twenty-first century competencies or skills. Conversations about the need for nurturing future-oriented abilities and aptitudes cannot be conclusive when we are often talking about different things but using the same words (Dede, 2010; Chalkiadaki, 2018; Joynes et al., 2019). Within different models of twenty-first century competencies, some of the elements referred to may include:

- critical thinking and divergent thinking
- communication skills
- team working
- autonomy and self-direction
- information and communications technology (ICT) proficiency
- emotion regulation skills
- problem solving, including adaptability
- creativity, including curiosity and playfulness
- mentalising (meta-cognition), learning how to think
- civic engagement
- global awareness, including cultural awareness (Chalkiadaki, 2018; Kim et al., 2019; Stehle & Peters-Burton, 2019).

Different ways of being a teacher, moving away from didactic delivery, and shifts in the curriculum away from facts and figures, are favoured by some across global education systems and here in the UK (Aynsley et al., 2012; Maker, 2022).

The 'knowledge economy' has been such that productivity is a measure of success, and success in school is measured against other schools and other education systems (Ball, 2021). In a changing world, having knowledge may no longer be as helpful as it has been. In challenging times, divergent thinking, curiosity, creativity, and the ability to work autonomously and as part of a team may become more valued. In current times, machines possess more knowledge than we could ever impart to a pupil at school (Russell, 2021). Young people live in this new world where information can be accessed when needed rather than stored and retrieved by their brains. They are used to outsourcing factual knowledge to their constant companion phones and tablets. Traditional qualifications for the old world of work and evidence of achievement in established curricular subjects may not be what modern employers are looking for (Tomlinson, 2001). Whether it is NASA asking prospective employees about their experience of playing with construction toys (Brown, 2009) or companies wanting to hear how job candidates have dealt with adversity, worked as part of a team, and had a Saturday job or paper round as indicators of potential for excellence (Greening, in BBC, 2021b), the criteria for job applications may be changing. Being resilient, creative, playful, and able to work in a team are part of labour market desirables that are developed by schools who address the whole child and seek to prepare them for life, both at work and at play.

Social progress for pupils and the nation

Education works as an agent of social progress when it addresses humanistic, civic, economic, and social development in equitable and just ways (IPSP, 2018). Elements seen across different frameworks for twenty-first century competencies develop both the personal and collective potential of pupils as well as prepare them for playing a part in the economic well-being of their community and wider global well-being. Social progress is achieved when both individuals become more equal and societies become more just. The Social Mobility Commission (2017) reported that less advantaged pupils in the UK continue to lag behind their more advantaged peers in attainment at school. This gap widens as pupils progress through their schooling and has been further negatively impacted by the COVID-19 pandemic (Social Mobility Commission, 2021). In the four nations of the UK, the Social Mobility Commission (2021) noted differences in the pace of response from each home nation in taking onboard their responsibility, as set out in the 2010 Equality Act (Legislation.gov.uk, 2010), to include social and economic implications of their decision-making. Scotland was the first home nation to enact this duty, with Wales also formally bringing this into legislation (Social Mobility Commission, 2021).

Ecclestone and Brunila (2015) feared that education settings may avoid acknowledging social inequalities and injustices and address the results of inequalities and injustice by teaching that seeks to manage or overcome behaviours and feelings engendered by external challenges. Not acknowledging inequality outside the school gates, while committing to providing equality in school, cannot address issues of social progress. During the pandemic, some pupils in disadvantaged areas experienced schools taking on the role of addressing need outside the school building, providing food, clothing, and resources for learning before addressing curriculum delivery. Recent unprecedented circumstances have clarified for many the need to meet basic needs before pupils will have an ability or desire to learn. Basic needs must be met before higher psychological needs for self-development and fulfilment matter (BPS, 2020). Giving pupils a level playing field for learning means ensuring that they are all fed, rested, warm, and safe. When education works for everyone, it can lead to a more equal and inclusive society; when education is unavailable, or only available to some, injustice and social exclusion are increased (IPSP, 2018).

Social progress through education could lead to dislocation for pupils who feel that change in them has alienated them from their roots or find that, in order to continue their progress, they must leave their community never to return. Rather than being an engine for positive social change, an education system that aims to increase prosperity can be a vehicle for perpetuating and replicating what already exists (Ball, 2021; Tomlinson, 2001). Visibility in neighbourhoods and a sense that education settings play an active part in the community are important for the sense that the school participates in, and adds positively to, the way the community functions (Kerr et al., 2016). Schools engaging with their community means social progress can be more inclusive and universal (Ainscow et al., 2012). Tomlinson (2001) felt that the shift of purpose for education in England from democratic public good in the post-war era to economic success in a globalised twenty-first century world has led to social justice being less prioritised in English education policy.

Economic growth of the nation

The Organisation for Economic Co-Operation and Development (OECD, 2021) advocated that knowledge and understanding are essential to the prosperity of all – outcomes of this knowledge and understanding being the ability to respond with agency and, when necessary, to bring about change. Ball (2021) saw government education policy in England as being driven by the desire to increase prosperity alongside a desire to make the country more equitable. Both Tomlinson (2001) and Ball (2021) appeared to agree that whether Conservative or Labour politicians have been in power, international economic advancement has been the purpose behind education policy-making. The first priority of the Department for Education (DfE) in 2021 was to 'drive economic growth through improving the skills pipeline, levelling up productivity and supporting people to work'. This might feel like an outdated objective for an education system for the future. It is hard to improve skills for the future if much of the school intake in the 2010s, 20s, and 30s may work in jobs that we have not yet seen or even thought of (Kirschner & Stoyanov, 2020; World Economic Forum, 2016). If the jobs are not as yet foreseen, the technologies not yet invented, or their applications not yet realised, and the exact nature of the challenges ahead are as yet unclear, teaching a future workforce to drive national economic growth will be a creative and imaginative undertaking (OECD, 2021; Schleicher, 2018; Vogel, 2015).

Contemporary concerns around issues such as inequality and climate change might drive a move away from a model of education as a foundation for the economic growth of the state. If we decide that the world cannot support constant economic growth because of the pressure on, and unjust distribution of, the natural resources of the planet, then education, like all other institutions, will need to adapt (OECD, 2018; Victor, 2010). Humans may be innately competitive, and the need to be ranked against others may never wane. A state's government can only be judged by some form of measurement, and calls to replace gross domestic product (GDP) as the measurement of success has grown in recent times. Whether it be the United Nations' (UN) Human Development Index (HDI) and Inclusive Wealth Index (IWI) or the UK's New Economic Foundation's Happy Planet Index (HPI), other measures have their supporters and their critics (Hawkes, 2021). If we were to move to a new measure of national success which includes economic health but preferences other areas of well-being, the first priority of education in England would likely move to mirror this.

The economic beliefs and tenets of a nation and the education system it supports have a two-way relationship. The education system is designed to support future economic well-being; the state of the nation's economy impacts the resourcing of the education system. Sometimes the economic realities of education spending by a nation state belies the rhetoric of policy from the political system in charge. The 'Levelling Up' agenda of the UK Conservative Government aimed to reverse inequalities and level up funding of schools (Johnson, 2021). A report from the Institute of Fiscal Studies judged that, in reality, there continued to be relatively larger funding cuts to the more deprived schools. In past budgets and in future forecasts, growth in budgets for the most advantaged schools was greater than that for the most disadvantaged (Sibieta, 2021).

Personal development of each pupil

Ronald Barnett (2012) foresaw a seismic shift in what we need from our education system in which the teaching of knowledge and skills would give way to a learning of what it is to be human. Stewart Russell, presenter of the BBC Reith Lectures 2021 on Artificial Intelligence, agreed that the future is a place where we will need to learn to be 'good at being human'. The future could be a place where we will move to thinking about how to make the most of life, and perhaps, we will be educated to live our best lives. These ideas about learning how to live and how to be suggest that somewhere, at some time, we have lost the art of being human. Fromm (1993) saw our spiritual, human 'being' as having been threatened by economic systems based around 'having'. The future may be about 'getting back' to ourselves if 'progress' has taken us away from our own humanity. Spiel et al. (2018) acknowledged that, along with civic and economic responsibilities of education, there is a humanistic purpose to fully develop the potential of each individual and the group or community purpose for the good of all. The OECD (2021) saw future educators as being charged with helping pupils to develop their moral and ethical principles. To some, this may feel like a family and community responsibility in which school is one part of the bigger 'village that raises a child'.

'Soft skills', the kind of areas of personal and social development we address in social emotional learning (SEL) programmes in schools, may not be as readily replaced by technologies as more concrete skills or knowledge. In Robinson's (2017) terms, learning about our internal world may not go out of fashion anytime soon. Thinking about what goes on in our internal landscape and those of others, having insight into patterns in relationships and compassion for self and others as we inter-relate, and having strategies for regulating our emotions and supporting emotion regulation for others will help to create a safer and more equal world. When we feel safer and more valued, we feel better, and we will do better.

If future society can bring about social change in terms of equality, and if we shift away from our twentieth-century patterns of consumerism, then it is likely we will have more leisure time and less need to purpose our lives around providing for our basic physical needs and our consumerist aspirations. This may lead to an increasing desire to meet our needs for psychological well-being and spiritual and personal fulfilment (BPS, 2020). Our schools are likely to already have within their mission statements something along the lines of: 'we aim to help children to live "flourishing" lives' (Clarke, 2020). Successful education provision for the future can foster learners to become agents of change (OECD, 2018), and schools could nurture lives which will, by the way they are lived, make the world a better place (OECD, 2018).

What are teachers for?

Teachers are there to implement the education we have trusted our politicians to commission for us. Many researchers agree on one thing about teachers and teaching: that it is true that teachers are the most important and influential resource in an education system (for instance, Husbands & Pearce, 2012; McKnight et al., 2016; Robinson, 2017). We need to recognise and value teachers who do a great job, and identify and support teachers who would benefit from developing certain parts of their practice. What do we consider to be important aspects of teaching abilities and aptitudes, and how do we identify or measure them? We are more likely to measure whether a teacher is effective than whether they are good (Ko et al., 2016). The things that make you feel lucky that your child is in a particular teacher's class appear to be based on different values from those selected by education policy-makers. Good is subjective and generic; it is challenging to imagine the outcomes that could be measured to see who is 'good'. Coe et al. (2014) feared that measuring is often reductive and can be misleading. Once we restrict the magical fairy dust quality of the teacher–pupil relationship into measurable items, the magic will evaporate, and we will lose the essence of the qualities we are hoping to assess (Gossman, 2011). Delors (1996) previously warned that attempting to define or to measure how a teacher influences the life and the future of their pupils can lead to not only missing the point but also potentially wrongly ascribing benefits in an attempt to isolate characteristics which, once determined, could be replicated. In education, measurements are often used in order to make improvements; if good teachers are born, knowing what makes one could help us to attract the right candidates into the profession but that may not mean we can train teachers how to be 'good'.

Creating categories of characteristics that conflate to create a 'good' teacher would require pupil voice to ensure the 'menu' captured the magic. Teacher characteristics praised by pupils, when asked about their favourite teacher, included goofy, funny, and comfortable (Woolf, 2016). Fun was often cited as a memorable and likeable quality, as well as being conducive to learning. Playful, humorous people with a warm energy inspire us. Appearance and dress were also linked to memorable positive teacher attributes – being stylish and cool was appreciated by pupils (Woolf, 2016). Being 'fun' and 'cool' might be engaging elements of what it is to be 'good' that would not make a scholarly list of valuable qualities.

Stakeholders' beliefs about what an effective teacher should be differ from the attributes identified by policy-makers (Gossman, 2011; McKnight et al., 2016). Desirable characteristics for effective teaching include having good knowledge of content and being able to effectively deliver the content, as well as knowing how to assess progress (Coe et al., 2014). Research indicates that consulting with pupils enhances the efficacy of teaching (Husbands & Pearce, 2012). An analysis of anecdotal stories in *The Times Educational Supplement* (Gossman, 2011) identified that the best teachers were committed, respectful, positive, encouraging, and inspirational.

What teachers are for may be changing; indeed, this will inevitably change as we repurpose the type of education we offer. Niu et al. (2021) drew together a list of twenty-first century competencies from a variety of models they reviewed. These contemporary competencies for teachers, similar to competencies to be fostered in pupils, were in technology, relationships, creativity, criticality, and autonomy. Pupils will benefit from teachers who engage with local and global citizenship and civic responsibility (Niu et al., 2021), just as schools make a difference in their communities through social and civic engagement. In a world that may turn our desire to teach on its head, good teaching may look different. If delivery of content and knowledge becomes a task for machines, as envisaged by Russell (2021), human teachers would gain more time to connect and offer compassion and emotional containment for children and young people (CYP).

Professional expectations of teachers

The Teachers Standards in England were published in 2011, with minor updates in 2013 and 2021. The DfE required staff to:

- develop good relationships with pupils
- use considered authority appropriately and firmly
- develop relationships of mutual respect
- maintain appropriate professional boundaries.

In Wales, the 2019 'Code of Professional Conduct and Practice for Registrants with the Education Workforce Council (EWC)' echoed expectations for respectful relationships and professional boundaries in schools. The EWC (2019) reminded their workforce that they are public servants and that, in order to maintain public trust and confidence, the members of the workforce are expected to take seriously their responsibilities as role models. To fulfil their role, staff should create just and inclusive spaces for learning that are likely to develop autonomy and poise in pupils. Teachers are there to provide a relationship within which learning and growth are fostered and curiosity, creativity, kindness, teamwork, and autonomy have space to flourish.

Being a reflective practitioner

The EWC (2020) offered a helpful template for questioning our practice in terms of how we relate to pupils. In order to understand whether we are acting appropriately within our professional boundaries, we should reflect on whether, if a colleague or member of the public were present, we would alter our behaviour. Reflecting on whether an observer might consider our behaviour to be inappropriate is a helpful way to gain perspective. If we consider whether, observing this behaviour in a colleague's interaction with a pupil, we would judge it to be inappropriate, that information will inform our practice. If we would behave differently, were we being observed, then it is likely that we need to rethink our interactions to ensure the safety of our pupils and the integrity of our profession.

In school, we are not a parent, friend, or therapist; when not in a teaching role, it might be helpful to think of our helping role as being more like the role of a mentor (Goldner & Mayseless, 2008). The 'Royal College of Nursing toolkit for nurses who are not mental health specialists' (2014) reminded us that we can offer more than a chat, but that we must be aware that we are not offering therapy. If we are self-aware, we will notice if we seem to stray into the role of parent, friend, or counsellor with certain pupils. Only if we know it can we choose to change it. Self-awareness and personal insight are key to professional practice in our relationships with pupils and more generally in our work role and workplaces.

Self-awareness in the role of teacher and worker in education

Self-awareness helps us to see the impacts of pupils on us and of us on pupils. In their work with focus groups of school staff, Kourkoutas and Giovazolias (2015) found that we are not always alert to the impact our pupil's behaviours or ways of interacting have on us. They noted practitioners with more general self-awareness had a better understanding of the impact of students on their feelings and behaviours.

There is a growing consensus that school staff would benefit from training in self-awareness and from support to have more reflection time in order to better understand students' behaviours and their underlying emotional needs. Increased self-awareness would also help teachers to reflect on their reactions or responses to pupils (Austin, 2010; Barnado's Scotland, 2020; Kourkoutas & Giovazolias, 2015; Rowe & Sturt, 2018). Insightful practitioners can perceive how pupils' needs, emotions, and behaviours lead to the experience of strong feelings and to reactions that may not always be helpful. Without insight and self-awareness in the adult, who is then able to adjust responses in the light of understanding, these interactions can become a negative cycle of distrust, dislike, and stress on both sides.

Self-awareness is absolutely not about a fault-finding perspective of our deficits. In academic terms, 'critical' means an unbiased analysis rather than the use of the word as meaning negatively judgemental. Self-awareness is helpful when accompanied by self-acceptance or compassion for self. When we use helping skills, such as active listening, we note and verbalise what we see and hear but do not judge or nudge toward change. When we give more thought to reflection on our own ways of relating and responding it is about noting, bringing into our conscious awareness the things that we experience, think, and feel. Whether we choose to change then becomes possible. Change itself is not the aim of self-reflection; professionalism and improving well-being are the goals, although beneficial change, for self and for others, may well be outcomes.

Taking on more in our role as educators in school feels like a big ask at a time when we know we have had to take on so many more ways of working and are being asked to provide academic 'catch up' time and activities. The Teacher Well-being Index, from Education Support (2020), a UK charity to support mental health and well-being for those working in education, reported that, in 2020, the experience of stress had grown for the third year running. Symptoms of this stress in the well-being index include tearfulness, sleep difficulties, and difficulty concentrating. The effects of stress were reported by staff in both physical and psychological symptoms, which often feed into negative behaviour patterns. It appears that school staff are experiencing times when their work situations take them outside of their window of tolerance. Suffering increasing anxiety suggests that teachers are experiencing hyper-arousal, while teachers who are increasingly experiencing low mood or feelings of depression indicates hypo-arousal. The Education Support (2020) findings suggest that work in schools has led to teachers' window of tolerance being exceeded in ways that have significantly impacted their mental health. In 2021, the Education Support survey found that, although improvements had been achieved in raising staff awareness of sources of well-being support, the levels of stress continued to be high and that this level of anxiety is unsustainable.

Without asking more in terms of time or actions, offering more in terms of knowledge and understanding could decrease rather than increase levels of stress for us in classrooms and schools. Developing theories in counselling and therapy practice suggest that understanding ourselves and understanding how the mind and body work are helpful in restoring better mental health. Mentalising, or understanding mental states in ourselves and others, is a key component in many healing approaches in mental health services (Bateman & Fonagy, 2019). Teaching knowledge about physical and emotional processes, sometimes referred to as psycho-education, is also increasingly recognised as helpful and used as part of therapeutic interventions for individuals, families, and groups (Burhouse et al., 2015; Higgins et al., 2020; Hood et al., 2021; Jeannotte et al., 2021). 'Know your enemy' can be an empowering approach; learning about the things we feel and think that cause us harmful physiological and social symptoms can shift our perceptions, even helping us to accept that the thoughts and feelings can be our friends. Once we learn to tune into information from all our parts– our bodies, minds, guts, and spirits – we can work out whether the messages are helpful or are not actually relevant in that moment.

Identifying the difference between what we wish we could do and what we practically and professionally are able to do can help us to understand the source of stress in situations when we want to make everything better but are unable to do so (Gunn, n.d.). Doing what you can and letting go of what you would like to do, or feel you should do, is important for your well-being. Remembering Donald Winnicott's (1974) advice that 'being good enough' is a helpful way to be, and accepting this as a truth, is good for our mental health in all areas of our lives. It is not a case of 'I *only* have to be good enough'; it means 'I *am* good enough and that is plenty'.

Natalie Davey (2020) suggested that 'The Good Enough Teacher' is one who can balance enough care and not too much care for their students, allowing them to feel secure and develop autonomy. They are the teacher who can create a healthy balance of care for students with care for self. If you have ever read Dr Seuss's (2003) *Oh, the Places You'll Go!*, you will be familiar with ideas of life as an ongoing balancing act. When we accept life's challenges for what they are, or when we are able to 'let it go', the way forward, or out, becomes clearer.

The golden rule

'Do as you would be done by' is a value we may try to live by. This should include 'do to yourself as you do to others'. In school, we are charged with developing health in students by providing for healthy eating and physical activity. Many schools include mindfulness as a provision, and we encourage families to ensure their children's healthy sleeping patterns. Eating healthily, sleeping well, and taking physical activity are all important and evidence-based parts of self-care. Mindfulness, the experience of being out in green spaces, and the role of pets in mental health promotion are all subjects of research and have been seen to offer positive benefits for good mental health. Part of the balancing act of work and non-work life is finding time for doing the things that *you* know work for you in changing your physical and emotional state.

We need knowledge, including, importantly, knowledge of ourselves, our histories, our current issues, our strengths, and our challenges if we are to use the power of our position fairly. Professional work includes using your knowledge and skills to build relationships and to support the whole development of those in our care. Being professional includes use of judgement in how we carry out our role within the contractual responsibilities and the legal frameworks of the position. While being professional, remember to also be yourself. If we are a role model for our pupils, it must surely include modelling what it is to be good at being human and how to be good at the art of living. Being genuine and authentic, being the one everyone says is 'comfortable in their own skin', models that being who you are is being good enough. Providing professional care and being an open and insightful practitioner helps us to provide the safe space for pupils to learn and to develop a secure sense of self.

School as a safe space and safe spaces in schools

Schools are for the provision of education and a place where CYP are safe to learn and to grow. We have learned a lot about the importance of school for pupils and for their communities during the COVID-19 pandemic. The experience of school closures has offered an opportunity to understand what we miss when schools are not there for us. Longer school days, breakfast clubs, and after school clubs all mean families missed a multi-provision of care as well as education when schools were shut. Increases in CYP being at risk and coming to harm during lockdowns may have been, in part, due to schools and others not being able to see any early-warning signs of harm. Pupils and families will also have experienced the loss of social connection and trusted adult support (Romanou & Belton, 2020). Exploitation of CYP may also have increased while they were out of school, some spending more time outside the home on the streets. The two million CYP who were already at risk in their home environment prior to COVID-19 were denied the 'safe haven' of school. Being at home all the time also extended the time of their exposure to risk of physical and psychological harm (Lewis et al., 2021).

Not being in school over the pandemic lockdown periods may have increased risk of harm to many, and led to more actual harm to some (Loiseau et al. 2021; Pereda & Diaz-Faes, 2020; Sidpra et al. 2021). School is a safe haven for some and a place of resources such as food and heating for others (Ambrose et al., 2021; Human Rights Watch (HRW), 2020), and it should be a safe experience for all. Experiencing school as a safe place to be sounds like something those in schools, and out of schools, should be able to take for granted. It is sad to hear, and gives us cause for reflection, that not insubstantial numbers of pupils felt safer at home during lockdowns and were anxious about the return to their schools (Mental Health Foundation 2021). Making school feel safe for all is one of the most important issues we need to address.

The sense of being safe in the classroom enhances the ability to learn (Holley & Steiner, 2005). This finding supports the need for us to create containment in classrooms and feelings of safety in schools. What that safety is, and what it means, requires some unpacking. Who is safe, how they are safe, whether safety is always a positive experience for everyone: these are ideas that are up for discussion (Flensner & Von der Lippe, 2019). Research in Scandinavian education settings considered the inherent dilemma of safe places: the need for freedom and openness of expression for the individual versus the need for respect and understanding for others and tolerance of *their* free and open expression (Flensner and Von der Lippe, 2019). Successful provision of a safe classroom means offering an environment where it is safe to take risks, to dare, and to have courage.

Having an area designated as a 'safe space' in school could suggest to pupils and parents that other spaces in school are not safe. Being specific with language, we might designate 'safe spaces' in schools as different, both in purpose and in provision, from school being a safe place for all. Some of us, at some times, need a space of retreat from the rest of school. This could be emotional retreat from the stress of work or the stress of relationships. It could also be a sanctuary from the sensory overwhelm of general school environments. In these retreat spaces, students can expect consistent, non-challenging experiences. These spaces do not have the same conflicting roles of stretch versus security but, rather, are for meeting the needs of those with sensory or social and emotional need for a refuge. This designated sanctuary is a location for regrouping and soothing from particular stressors or for times of particular vulnerability.

The two different containment roles for safe schools and designated safe spaces can be understood through Barry Mason's (2019) model of safe uncertainty. There are four main positions of safety, or lack of it, in Mason's model: safe certainty, safe uncertainty, unsafe certainty, and unsafe uncertainty. Although the last two ideas may sound unappealing, as humans, we often fear uncertainty more than lack of safety and may seek certainty, even though it could be a dangerous place to be. In terms of safe spaces in education, safe certainty is a description of withdrawal spaces in school. When we are depleted of resilience, these places offer safety and consistent, predictable environments without challenge or disagreement. In whole school environments, Flensner and Von der Lippe (2019) argued that safe certainty would not allow for key aspects of teaching and learning, such as challenge, expression of different views, and controversy. Safe schools need to offer safe uncertainty – places where pupils feel safe to explore their external and internal worlds and safe enough to be themselves, try out being other, and choose to change. Callan (2016) wrote of being 'intellectually unsafe' as an important experience in education, but this is accompanied by the requirement that all present be civil and open to differences and to not always feeling comfortable. The language of civility, dignity, and bravery or courage describe spaces where tolerance and respect accompany challenge and stretch. Safe schools and classrooms, built on safe uncertainty, do not promise an easy time. Uncertainty is often a place of discomfort for humans but also an opportunity for excitement, exploration, development of resilience, and personal growth. The safety to be heard, respected, and make mistakes or not know the answer is the most important right of pupils in our education settings (Murdoch et al., 2020). Balancing this with the expectation of respect, curiosity, and kindness toward others creates a place where it feels safe to be oneself.

Conclusion

The literature suggests schools and teachers fulfil many functions. The beliefs and understandings of the purpose of education have changed as societies' needs and political and philosophical thinkers have shifted. The requirement that schools instruct, enlighten, inform, and develop CYP has remained a core purpose and responsibility of schools. Different groups give different significance to various areas of an expanded school curricular and extra-curricular provisions. An education system is situated within the cultural and political traditions of time and of place. Being able to remember facts and figures had historical importance; this has been added to, or possibly superseded by, the value accorded to being able to discriminate, process, and apply information. The teaching of arts or of sciences may appear to be favoured at different points in our histories. As the school curricula in the UK became more homogenised across school settings, teaching of personal and social skills and well-being were included in the syllabus. Schools became places with a mission to nurture a more holistic development of talents and skills. The remit for education also moved to ensuring the physical health and well-being of pupils as well as their social inclusion and emotional well-being.

Education and schools change in response to the needs of their stakeholders. Schools nurture pupils to become agents of change that will benefit their society as well as themselves. Burgeoning technologies, novel opportunities, and emerging challenges compel schools to adapt and adjust at a greater speed than previously experienced. The curriculum may change, requiring us to learn, ourselves, what it is we need to teach and comprehend the evolution of knowledge and understanding that we want to foster in our pupils. Further responsibilities will include acknowledging the impact of injustices in historical, cultural, social and geo-political histories, while containing our anxieties around predictions for the future, and uncertainty about the present in order to provide emotional containment for our pupils in challenging times.

References

Ainscow, M., Dyson, A., Goldrick, S. and West, M. (2012) Making schools effective for all: Rethinking the task. *School Leadership & Management*, 32 (3), 197–213.

Ambrose, A., Baker, W., Sheriff, G. and Chambers, J. (2021) Cold comfort: Covid-19, lockdown and the coping strategies of fuel poor households. *Energy Reports*, 7 (November), 5589–5596. Available from: doi: 10.1016/j.egyr.2021.08.175

Austin, D. (2010) Consultancy supervision in schools. *Emotional and Behavioural Difficulties Journal*, June, 15 (2), 125–139.

Aynsley, S., Brown, C. and Sebba, J. (2012) *Opening Minds: An Evaluative Literature Review*. London: Royal Society of Arts (RSA). Available from: https://www.thersa.org/globalassets/rsa-om-literature-review.pdf [Accessed 13th June 2021].

Ball, S. (2021) *The Education Debate*. 4th ed. Bristol: Policy Press.

Barnardo's Scotland (2020) Supervision in education: Healthier schools for all. Available from: https://www.barnardos.org.uk/sites/default/files/uploads/Supervision%20in%20Education%20-%20Healthier%20Schools%20For%20All%20-%20Main%20report_0.pdf [Accessed 27th October 2021].

Barnett, R. (2012) Learning for an unknown future. *Higher Education Research and Development*, February, 31 (1), 65–77.

Bateman, A. and Fonagy, P. (eds.) (2019) *Handbook of Mentalizing in Mental Health Practice*. 2nd ed. Washington, DC: American Psychiatric Publishing, Inc.

BBC (2021a) Loosening the old school tie. *Radio 4*, 14 December. Available from: https://www.bbc.co.uk/sounds/play/m00121wr [Accessed 17th December 2021].

BBC (2021b) Technology and education. Rethink education, Episode 5. *Radio 4*, 9th July. Available from: https://www.bbc.co.uk/sounds/play/m000xmyz [Accessed 04th September 2021].

Bellanca, J. and Brandt, R. (eds.) (2010) *21st Century Skills: Rethinking How Students Learn.* Bloomington: Solution Tree Press.

British Psychological Society (BPS) (2020) Emotionally regulate before we educate: Focusing on psychological wellbeing in the approach to a new school day. *BRE33v*, 14 August. Available from: https://www.bps.org.uk/sites/www.bps.org.uk/files/Policy/Policy%20-%20Files/Psychological%20wellbeing%20in%20the%20approach%20to%20a%20new%20school%20day%20%28DECP%20NI%29.pdf [Accessed 11th June 2021].

Brown, S. (2009) *Play: How it Shapes the Brain, Opens the Imagination and Invigorates the Soul.* New York: Avery.

Burhouse, A., Rowland, M., Niman, H., Abraham, D. Collins, E., Matthews, H. Denney, J. and Ryland, H. (2015) Coaching for recovery: A quality improvement project in mental healthcare. *BMJ Open Quality*, 4 (1). Available from: doi: 10.1136/bmjquality.u206576.w2641 [Accessed 23rd May 2022].

Callan, E. (2016) Education in safe and unsafe spaces. *Philosophical Inquiry in Education*, 24 (1), 64–78.

Chalkiadaki, A. (2018) A systematic literature review of 21st century skills and competencies in primary education. *International Journal of Instruction*, July, 11 (3), 1–16. Available from: doi: 10.12973/iji.2018.1131a

Clarke, T. (2020) Children's wellbeing and their academic achievement: The dangerous discourse of 'trade-offs' in education. *Theory and Research in Education*, 18 (3), 263–294.

Coe, R., Aloisi, C., Higgins, S. & Major, L. (2014) What makes great teaching? Review of the underpinning research. *The Sutton Trust.* Available from: https://www.suttontrust.com/wp-content/uploads/2014/10/What-Makes-Great-Teaching-REPORT.pdf [Accessed 11th December 2021].

Davey, N. (2020) The good enough teacher. *The Journal of the Assembly for Expanded Perspectives on Learning*, 25 (7), 157–172.

Dede, C. (2010) Comparing frameworks for 21st century skills. In: Bellanca, J., & Brandt, R. (eds.) *21st Century Skills: Rethinking How Students Learn.* Bloomington: Solution Tree Press. 51–76.

Delors, J. (1996) *Learning, the Treasure Within: Report to UNESCO of the International Commission on Education for the Twenty-First Century.* Paris: UNESCOPub.

Department for Education (DfE) (2011) Teachers' standards: Guidance for school leaders, school staff and governing bodies. Available from: https://www.gov.uk/government/publications/teachers-standards#history [Accessed 28th August 2021].

Department for Education (DfE) (2021) Outcome delivery plan: 2021 to 2022. 15 July. Available from: https://www.gov.uk/government/publications/department-for-education-outcome-delivery-plan/dfe-outcome-delivery-plan-2021-to-2022 [Accessed 01st December 2021].

Department for Education (NI) (n.d.) Education transformation programme. Available from: https://www.education-ni.gov.uk/topics/education-transformation-programme [Accessed 01st December 2021].

Ecclestone, K. & Brunila, K. (2015) Governing emotionally vulnerable subjects and 'therapisation' of social justice, *Pedagogy, Culture & Society*, 23 (4), 485–506.

Education Support (2020) *Teacher Well-being Index 2020.* London: Education Support. Available from: https://www.educationsupport.org.uk/media/yfrhfjca/teacher_wellbeing_index_2020.pdf [Accessed 11th August 2021].

Education Support (2021) *Teacher Well-being Index 2021.* London: Education Support. Available from: https://www.educationsupport.org.uk/resources/for-organisations/research/teacher-wellbeingindex/?gclid=CjwKCAiAtouOBhA6EiwA2nLKH_d0qfhx30OeTi9LvFFXlW4l3NkCLaJ3AinPEnKeyUgFcpySNIbh5hoCY5EQAvD_BwE [Accessed 18th January 2022].

Education Workforce Council (2019) Code of professional conduct and practice for registrants with the Education Workforce Council (EWC). Available from: https://www.ewc.wales/site/index.php/en/fitness-to-practise/code-of-professional-conduct-and-practice-pdf.html [Accessed 17th December 2021].

Education Workforce Council (EWC) (2020) Maintaining professional boundaries with learners. https://www.ewc.wales/site/index.php/en/46-english/ftp/good-practice-guides/1385-guide-to -good-practice-in-maintaining-professional-boundaries-with-learners.html [Accessed 17th December 2021].

Flensner, K. and Von der Lippe, M. (2019) Being safe from what and safe for whom? A critical discussion of the conceptual metaphor of 'safe space'. *Intercultural Education* 30 (3), 275–288.

Fromm, E. (1993) *The Art of Being Human*. London: Constable.

Gibb, N. (2021) The importance of a knowledge-rich curriculum. Speech to a Social Marketing Foundation panel event on raising school standards. 21 July. Available from: https://www.gov .uk/government/speeches/the-importance-of-a-knowledge-rich-curriculum [Accessed 20th January 2022]. Open Government Licence v3.0. OGL. Full details available at: https://www .nationalarchives.gov.uk/doc/open-government-licence/version/3/

Goldner, L. and Mayselees, O. (2008) Juggling the roles of parents, therapists, friends and teachers: A working model for an integrative conception of mentoring. *Mentoring & Tutoring: Partnership in Learning*, 16 (4), 412–428. Available from: doi: 10.1080/13611260802433783

Gossman, P. (2011) My best teacher. *Teacher Education Advancement Network Journal*, 3 (1). Available from: https://insight.cumbria.ac.uk/1344/1/Gossman_MyBestTeacher.pdf [Accessed 04th December 2021].

Gunn, J. (n.d.) Self-care for teachers of traumatized students. *Resilient Educator*. Available from: https://resilienteducator.com/classroom-resources/self-care-for-teachers/ [Accessed 08th December 2021].

Hawkes, H. (2021) GDP alternatives: 8 Ways of measuring economic health. *In The Black*, 6 September. Available from: https://www.intheblack.com/articles/2021/09/06/8-ways-of -measuring-economic-health [Accessed 27th November 2021].

Higgins, A., Murphy, R., Downes, C. Barry, J., Monahan, M. Hevey, D., Kroll, T., Doyle, L. & Gibbons, P. (2020) Factors impacting the implementation of a psychoeducation intervention within the mental health system: A multisite study using the consolidation framework for implementation research. *BMC Health Services Research*, 9 November, 20 (1023). Available from: doi: 10.1186/s12913-020-05852-9

Holley, L. & Steiner, S. (2005) Safe space: Student perspectives on classroom environment. *Journal of Social Work Education*, Winter, 41 (1), 49–64.

Hood, B., Jelbert, S. and Santos, L. (2021) Benefits of a psychoeducational happiness course on university student mental well-being both before and during a COVID-19 lockdown. *Health Psychology Open*, January. Available from: doi: 10.1177/2055102921999291

Human Rights Watch (HRW) (2020) UK: Children in England going hungry with schools shut. Uneven UK approach for Covid-19 doesn't guarantee Children's right to food. 27 May. Available from: https://www.hrw.org/news/2020/05/27/uk-children-england-going-hungry -schools-shut [Accessed 17th December 2021].

Husbands, C. and Pearce, J. (2012) *What Makes Great Pedagogy? Nine Claims from Research*. Nottingham: National College for School Leadership.

International Panel on Social Progress (IPSP) (2018) *Rethinking Society for the 21st Century*. Cambridge: Cambridge University Press.

Jeannotte, A., Hutchinson, D. and Kellerman, G. (2021) Time to change for mental health and well-being via virtual professional coaching: Longitudinal observational study. *Journal of Medical Internet Research*, 23 (7), e27774. Available from: doi: 10.2196/27774

Johnson, B. (2021) The Prime Minister's levelling up speech. 15 July. Available from: https://www .gov.uk/government/speeches/the-prime-ministers-levelling-up-speech-15-july-2021 [Accessed 16th December 2021].

Joynes, C., Rossignoli, S. and Amonoo-Kuofi, E. (2019) 21st Century skills: Evidence of issues in definition, demand and delivery for development contexts. *Emerging Issues Report, Education Development Trust*. Available from: https://assets.publishing.service.gov.uk/media/5d71187 ce5274a097c07b985/21st_century.pdf [Accessed 24th July 2021].

Kerr, K., Dyson, A. and Gallannaugh, F. (2016) Conceptualising school-community relations in disadvantaged neighbourhoods: Mapping the literature. *Educational Research*, 58(3), 265–282.

Kim, S., Raza, M. and Seidman, E. (2019) Improving 21st-century teaching skills: The key to effective 21st-century learners. *Research in Comparative and International Education*, 14 (1), 99–117. Available from: doi: 10.1177/1745499919829214

Kirschner, P. A., and Stoyanov, S. (2020) Educating youth for non-existent/not yet existing professions. *Educational Policy*, 34 (3), 477–517.

Ko, J., Sammons, P. and Bakkum, L. (2016) *Effective Teaching*. Reading: Education Development Trust.

Kourkoutasa, E. and Giovazolias, T. (2015) School-based counselling work with teachers: An integrative model. *The European Journal of Counselling Psychology*, 3 (2), 137–158.

Legislation.gov.uk. (2010) Equality Act 2010. [online] Available from: http://www.legislation.gov.uk/ukpga/2010/15/contents [Accessed 11th September 2021].

Lewis, S., Munro, A., Smith, G. and Pollock, A. (2021) Closing schools is not evidence based and harms children. *BMJ*, 23 (February), 372 (521). Available from: doi: 10.1136/bmj.n521

Loiseau, M., Cottenet, J., Bechraoui-Quantin, S., Gilard-Pioc, S., Mikaeloff, Y., Jollant, F., François-Purssell, I., Jud, A. & Quantin C. (2021) Physical abuse of young children during the COVID-19 pandemic: Alarming increase in the relative frequency of hospitalizations during the lockdown period. *Child Abuse & Neglect*, December, 122, 105299. Available from: doi: 10.1016/j.chiabu.2021.105299.

Maker, C. (2022) From leading to guiding, facilitating, and inspiring: A needed shift for the 21st century. *Education Sciences*, 12 (18). Available from: doi: 10.3390/educsci12010018

Mason, B. (2019) Re-visiting safe uncertainty: Six perspectives for clinical practice and the assessment of risk. *Journal of Family Therapy*, 41 (3), 343–356.

McKnight, K., Graybeal, L., Yarbo, J. and Graybeal, J. (2016) England: What makes an effective teacher? Pearson. Available from: https://www.pearson.com/content/dam/corporate/global/pearson-dot-com/files/innovation/global-survey/reports/RINVN9283_UK_July_090516.pdf [Accessed 11th September 2021].

Mental Health Foundation (2021) The challenge facing schools and pupils. 04th March. Available from: https://www.mentalhealth.org.uk/coronavirus/returning-school-after-lockdown/challenge-facing-schools-pupils [Accessed 23rd January 2022].

Murdoch, D., English, A., Hintz, A. and Tyson, K. (2020) Feeling heard: Inclusive education, transformative learning, and productive struggle. *Educational Theory*, 70 (5), 653–679.

Niu, S., Niemi, H., Harju, V. and Pehkonen, L. (2021) Finnish student teachers' perceptions of their development of 21st-century competencies. *Journal of Education for Teaching*, 47 (5), 638–653.

Organisation for Economic Co-operation and Development (OECD) (2018) Social and emotional skills: Well-being connectedness and success. Available from: http://www.oecd.org/education/school/UPDATED%20Social%20and%20Emotional%20Skills%20-%20Well-being,%20connectedness%20and%20success.pdf%20(website).pdf [Accessed 25th November 2021].

Organisation for Economic Co-operation and Development (OECD) (2021) Building the future of education. Available from: https://www.oecd.org/education/future-of-education-brochure.pdf [Accessed 04th January 2022].

Pereda, N. and Díaz-Faes, D. (2020) Family violence against children in the wake of COVID-19 pandemic: A review of current perspectives and risk factors. *Child and Adolescent Psychiatry and Mental Health*, 14 (40). Available from: doi: 10.1186/s13034-020-00347-1

Robinson, K. (2017) Sir Ken Robinson compares human organisations to organisms: Education is a dynamic system. 3 April. Available from: https://hundred.org/en/articles/5-sir-ken-robinson-compares-human-organisations-to-organisms-education-is-a-dynamic-system [Accessed 04th January 2022].

Romanou, E. and Belton, E. (2020) *Isolated and Struggling: Social Isolation and the Risk of Child Maltreatment, in Lockdown and Beyond*. London: NSPCC.

Rowe, J. and Sturt, P. (2018) Using supervision in schools: A guide to building safe cultures and providing emotional support in a range of school settings. Shoreham-by-Sea, West Sussex: Pavilion.

Royal College of Nursing (2014) Mental health in children and young people: An RCN toolkit for nurses who are not mental health specialists. Available from: https.rcn.org.uk/media/octoberPUB-003311.pdf [Accessed 19th November 2021].

Russell, S. (2021) AI and the Economy. *BBC Reith Lectures. Living With Artificial Intelligence.* Lecture 3, Edinburgh. 15 December. Available from: https://www.bbc.co.uk/programmes/m0012fnc [Accessed 04th January 2022].

Seuss (2003) *Oh, The Places You'll Go.* London: Harper Collins.

Schleicher, A. (2018) Educating learners for their future, not our past. *ECNU Review of Education*, March, 1 (1), 58–75.

Scruton, R. (2016) What's the point of education. Available from: https://www.roger-scruton.com/articles/384-what-s-the-point-of-education-spectator-life-nov-16 [Accessed 11th July 2021].

Sibieta, L. (2021) School spending in England: Trends over time and future outlook. *The Institute for Fiscal Studies*, September. Available from: https://ifs.org.uk/uploads/BN334-School-spending-in-England-trends-over-time-and-future-outlook.pdf [Accessed 21st December 2021].

Sidpra, J., Abomeli, D., Hameed, B., Baker, J. and Mankad, K. (2021) Rise in the incidence of abusive head trauma during the COVID-19 pandemic. *Archives of Disease in Childhood*, 106 (3). Available from: doi: 10.1136/archdischild-2020-319872

Smith, E. (2018) *Key Issues in Education and Social Justice.* 2nd ed. London: Sage.

Social Mobility Commission (2017) Time for change: An assessment of Government policies on social mobility 1997–2017. Available from: https://assets.publishing.service.gov.uk/government/uploads/system/uploads/attachment_data/file/622214/Time_for_Change_report_-_An_assessement_of_government_policies_on_social_mobility_1997-2017.pdf [Accessed 14th September 2021].

Social Mobility Commission (2021) State of the nation 2021: Social mobility and the pandemic. Available from: https://assets.publishing.service.gov.uk/government/uploads/system/uploads/attachment_data/file/1003977/State_of_the_nation_2021_-_Social_mobility_and_the_pandemic.pdf [Accessed 20th January 2022].

Spiel, C., Schwartzman, S., Busemeyer, M., Cloete, N., Drori, G., Lassnigg, L., Schober, B., Schweisfurth, M., Verma, S. and Reich, R. (2018) The contribution of education to social progress. In: International Panel on Social Progress (IPSP) (ed.) *Rethinking Society for the 21st Century: Report of the International Panel on Social Progress.* Cambridge: Cambridge University Press. 753–778.

Stehle, S. and Peters-Burton, E. (2019) Developing student 21st Century skills in selected exemplary inclusive STEM high schools. *The International Journal of STEM Education*, 6 (39). Available from: doi: 10.1186/s40594-019-0192-1

Tan, J., Choo, S., Kan, T. and Liem, G. (2017) Educating for twenty-first century competencies and future-ready learners: Research perspectives from Singapore. *Asia Pacific Journal of Education*, 37 (4), 425–436.

Tomlinson, S. (2001) Education policy, 1997–2000: The effects on top, bottom and middle England. *International Studies in Sociology of Education*, 11 (3), 261–278. Available from: doi: 10.1080/09620210100200079

Victor, P. (2010) Questioning economic growth. *Nature*, 18 November, 468, 370–371. Available from: https://www.nature.com/articles/468370a [Accessed 11th July 2021].

Vogel, P. (2015) *Generation Jobless? Turning the Youth Unemployment Crisis into Opportunity.* London: Palgrave Macmillan.

Winnicott, D. (1974) *Playing and Reality.* Middlesex: Pelican Books.

Woolf, A. (2016) *Better Play: Practical Strategies for Supporting Play in Schools for Children of All Ages.* Driffield: Worth Publishing.

World Economic Forum (2016) The future of jobs employment, skills and workforce strategy for the fourth industrial revolution. Global Challenge Insight Report. Available from: https://www3.weforum.org/docs/WEF_Future_of_Jobs.pdf [Accessed 27th September 2021].

Conclusion

Schools can impart academic learning and, at the same time, instil pupils with a sense of their own worth and develop in them the capacity for living a personally fulfilling and socially constructive life. Having the knowledge that we need and the sense of meaning and purpose that we want are important strengths for maintaining and restoring good mental health.

Being a wise, compassionate, and containing teacher who builds connections with pupils, working in a school that fosters a sense of belonging for all of its inhabitants and has a place in the heart of its community is not a panacea for all ills. Communities need responsive, fair, just, and well-resourced service providers, and to know that they have a voice both locally and nationally.

Schools employing the principles of cognition, compassion, containment, and connection may offer each pupil the possibility of better mental health, but it will not ensure good mental health for all at all times. The aim of the four principles is not to identify or target pupils for interventions but, rather, to offer positive, healthy relationships to all. We all have mental health – sometimes good, sometimes not so good. Knowing more about mental health and having warmth and acceptance for self and for others, alongside the intention to 'make things better', is about demonstrating our humanity – it is not about being a mental health responder. Having cognition of, and compassion for, our fellow humans and ourselves are key elements for developing and sustaining better mental health for pupils and teachers. Managing our emotional responses and containing the feelings of pupils in our classrooms by modelling, whenever possible, and by teaching helpful strategies, when necessary, is a professional responsibility. Providing emotional containment in the classroom can be a challenging responsibility for teachers. It is not something we could outsource to anyone else, but it is a key element of support for better mental health in schools.

The aim of *Better Mental Health in Schools: Four Key Principles for Practice in Challenging Times* is to empower teachers and schools to:

- understand more about mental health in their pupils
- understand more about the impact of their work on their own mental health
- feel more confident that they can be helpful
- develop informed practices that support mental health
- accept the limitations of their role in addressing chronic or acute mental health in pupils
- engage in productive discussions about referrals and sources of external support for pupil's mental health
- be prepared for the challenges ahead for the mental health of our children and young people (CYP).

DOI: 10.4324/9781003277903-8

Conclusion

The COVID-19 pandemic has caused us to re-evaluate education and school as community. It is part of the human condition to seek predictability, certainty, and safety. Experiencing a sudden, unexpected threat that brought change and the loss of choice, autonomy, and routine has been a 'wake-up call'. It has certainly helped us to focus on how to live life in challenging times. At the time we experienced the COVID-19 pandemic, our societies were growing more aware of changes we wanted and needed to make in order to address injustices and inequalities, past and present, while preparing for the global challenges ahead. Injustice, inequality, the exploitation of peoples, and of the natural world all may contain an element of generational conflict. My generation could be perceived as having created or ignored problems humanity now faces. Compassion and containment for ourselves and our pupils are going to be important in creating safe spaces in schools where teachers support their pupils as they wrestle with not only personal growth and development and how to contribute to their community but also the anxieties and opportunities for the world in which they want to play a useful part.

The future may bring threats to the mental health of younger generations, even existential threats of survival. The future will bring opportunities for being part of something, for finding purpose and meaning, and for a sense of belonging in a group with a shared goal. Challenge and stress can be good or bad for our mental health. Our capacity for resilience, the general state of our mental health, and our positive connections to others dictate the amount of challenge and stress we can meet with before our mental health might need professional support.

In schools, we can support the development of resilience and provide relationships and environments that nurture better mental health. Teachers are significant in the lives of their pupils and are there when pupils experience common fluctuations in their everyday mental and emotional well-being. For many pupils, developing better mental health and being supported through the ups and downs of emotional well-being may often be enough – whether their fluctuating state of mental health is a natural response to life events or an unconscious response to triggers not available to awareness. For other pupils, our role in school may be to 'hold' or sustain them as they wait for, and attend, specialist services.

Teachers' and pupils' increased knowledge and understanding of mental health can lead to better emotional well-being. Offering compassion and containment creates calm connected classrooms. There will always be a need for specialist mental health professionals to support CYP, alongside resourced schools supporting their pupils' well-being. The intention for *Better Mental Health in Schools: Four Key Principles for Practice in Challenging Times* chimes with the Welsh Government's (2021 p. 5) 'Framework on embedding a whole-school approach to emotional and mental wellbeing':

> It aims to address the emotional and mental well-being needs of **all** children and young people, as well as school staff, as part of the whole-school community. It also recognises that the school alone cannot meet all the needs of what is a complex population of young people, whose needs will vary as they progress through infancy to adolescence and early adulthood. It is not about medicalising well-being; rather it is about taking account of the continuum of need.

We absolutely need functioning and effective specialist mental health services available to pupils, whether based in or outside of schools. We also need to recognise, protect, and value the excellent resources we have inside school for developing and maintaining better mental health: our teachers.

References

Welsh Government (2021) Framework guidance on embedding a whole-school approach to mental health and wellbeing. Available from: https://gov.wales/sites/default/files/publications/2021-03/framework-on-embedding-a-whole-school-approach-to-emotional-and-mental-well-being.pdf [Accessed 19th December 2021] Open Government Licence v3.0. OGL. Full details available at: https://www.nationalarchives.gov.uk/doc/open-government-licence/version/3/

Index

academic progress: cognition and 27; and COVID-19 15, 106; emotion regulation and 68, 69, 74; and relationships with teachers 8, 13; sense of belonging in school 88, 92; stigma and *see* stigma

adolescence: attachment and 70; and COVID-19 15; emotion regulation 68–9; identity development 8; importance of compassion for 53, 54; and parents 84; peer relationships in 89; school belonging in 89; stigma in *see* stigma; teacher relationships in 89–90

Adverse Childhood Experiences 84

anxiety 28, 29, 39, 49; climate change 16; and role of compassion 48, 51; and COVID-19 17; negative impacts of 61; teachers' feelings of 6, 36, 107; *see also* emotion regulation

attachment: allo-attachment 31; behaviours 70, 81–2; insecure 52; and loss, 82-3; oxytocin and 53; para-attachment 31; secure 52, 70; and teacher styles 31, 32; theory of 27, 31–2, 80–1; *see also* emotion regulation

attendance 88; stigma and 7–8; sense of belonging and 88, 92

be a person as well as a teacher *71, 89–90*

being a reflective practitioner *105–6*

being with 50, 86

British Psychological Society (BPS) 10, 17, 74, 92, 102, 104

buffer: attachment as 84, 85; compassion as 53; peer relationships as 85; social buffering 84–5, 79

CAMHS *see* specialist mental health services

capable 29; and self-esteem 84; *see also* Crucial Cs

classroom dynamics 26–7; teacher-pupil 31, 87

climate change *see* anxiety

cognition 13; definition of 25; and resistance to change 26; social 25; in teachers' practice 26–8; theory of mind 25, 33

cognitive approaches to better mental health: and mental state talk 33–4; in pupils 32–6; in school staff 36–9

compassion 27–8, 45–55, 115; definition 45, 53; deserving of 48; difference from empathy 53; fatigue 48, 52; IFS and 46; for others 45; in pupils' mental health 53-4; for self 46; social role of 46–7; in teachers' mental health 52–3; in teachers' practice 49–52

competencies: curriculum 100–1; in teachers' practice 105–8

connection 15, 79–80; and attachment 53, 70, 80–3; in the community 14, 87; and human health and well-being 79; importance of social relationships 80; need for 28–9; play and 90–1; *see also* Crucial Cs; sense of belonging in school

containment 61–2; in the classroom 108–9; definition 61; holding environment 61; in relationship 70–4; *see also* emotion; emotion regulation; window of tolerance

cortisol 49, 79

count *see* Crucial Cs

courage and self-esteem 84; *see also* Crucial Cs

COVID-19 pandemic: fear of future pandemics 3, 15–16; impact of 5, 14, 115; inequalities and 14, 101–2; responding to 10, 15–16; school closures during 2, 108

Crucial Cs 28, 49; and attachment style 81; in supervision 39

Department for Education 17, 100, 102; eight principles for promoting mental health 14

development: basic needs 102; holistic 9, 17, 86, 101, 103–4, 110; link between mental well-being and cognitive 1; models of human 88; parenting skills in child 33, 66, 70, 73, 83; personal of each pupil 103–4; professional 26, 32, 37–8; *see also* professional standards

economic drivers of education provision 100–4

emotion: costs to teachers 10, 27, 52–3; definition of 62; good and bad 63; intelligence 32; and mental health 8, 9; mixed 64–5; number of 62–3; *see also* containment

119

Index

emotion regulation: in attachment relationships 31, 70–3; competence 65; definition of 65; development of 68–9, 70–1; enhancing in the classroom 66–9; explicit 65; implicit 65; relationships in schools and 71–2; stability 65; stages of 66; strategies for 66–9; teachers' 71–2; unhelpful strategies for 73–4

empathy: definition 53; and mentalisation 26; *see also* compassion

England: measure of national well-being 103; mental health curriculum in 14; mental health services for CYP in 9–10, 12, 13; numbers with mental health needs in 5, 6; school counselling in 11; vision of education in 91, 100, 102–3; youth justice in 7; *see also* teachers standards; Department for Education

family: beliefs 63, 70; relationships 70, 71, 83; parenting and attachment in 52; *see also* development parenting skills in child

fight and flight 47, 51, 69; and tend and befriend 47

Fonagy, P. 26, 36, 107

future: of education 99–104; emerging threats 15–16, 116; preparing for 16

good enough 83–4; *see also* teacher qualities

helping skills *see* therapeutic skills

inequality 16, 85, 116; in the community 102; social 87, 102; *see also* COVID-19

injustice 3, 16, 87, 102, 116; economic 17; historical and geo-political 3; social 87

intergenerational trauma 3

kindness: be kind movement 49; and compassion 48; and kinship 89

Klein, J. 61, 62, 79, 81

knowledge: led curriculum 100; and economy 101, 102; in future curriculum 103–5, 110

limitations to supporting mental health in schools 7, 115; funding 7, 12–13, 103; lack of confidence 6, 7, 9; lack of knowledge 12; lack of skills 9; staffing 7; training 12–13; workload 7, 13; *see also* cognition in teachers' practice

managing feelings *see* emotion regulation

mental health: acute or chronic 1, 10, 115; in the curriculum 9, 13, 14, 54, 107; identification of needs 2, 5, 7, 8, 11, 14, 17–18, 115; prevalence of poor 5–7; *see also* specialist services

Mental Health First Aid Training 6, 13

mental health support in schools 8-10; whole-school approach to mental health and well-being 9, 92, 116; front-line of 10–13, 17; school counselling service 11; government initiatives for 3, 13, 14

mentalisation 26, 30, 36–7, 39

NHS 5, 6, 17, 48, 74

normalising 27, 34, 39, 73; inherent challenges of growing up 13, 14

Northern Ireland: mental health budget in 6; school counselling in 11; curriculum in 14; prevalence of mental health needs in 15

parents 5, 7, 14, 17, 83, 84, 86; parenting skills 33, 70, 73; response to pandemic 15; *see also* family parenting and attachment

parts: emotions and 74; and inner conflict 64–5; Internal Family Systems (IFS) 46; psychology of 35; theory of 34-5, 37; *see also* play expressing parts

peer relationships 15, 28, 54; and sense of belonging 88, 91–2; and social buffering 85; as source of stress 85, 89; as support 38, 84–5; *see also* stigma from peers

play 69; and attachment 90; and bonding 90–1; expressing parts 35–6; and relational repair 90, 91

professional expectations of teachers 105–7; boundaries 105–6; Code of Professional Conduct and Practice for Registrants with the Education Workforce Council 105; teachers standards 26, 105

relationships *see* connection

resilience: belief of in pupils 14; development of 1, 13–15, 61, 72, 109, 116; and health benefits 80; lack of belief of in pupils 14, 54

responsibility for the mental health of CYP: discussion of 1, 17, 99–104; filling the gap 2, 10–13; picking up the pieces 17; schools as primary support 11; *see also* specialist services

safeguarding 12; *see also* teachers standards

safety: creating a sense of 3, 8, 13, 15, 27, 51; intellectually unsafe 109; Mason's model of safe uncertainty 109; schools as a safe space 108–9

schools: the point of 99–104; primary 11–12, 13; secondary 11, 54, 69, 90, 92

Scotland: curriculum for compassion and connection 54; equality legislation in 102; mental health training in 6, 14; school counselling in 11

self-awareness 51; and attachment 30–2, 81; in teachers 106–7 sense of belonging in school 88–9, 115; how to develop 89–92; importance of 15, 79, 85

social justice 46, 47, 87, 102

specialist services: access to 10, 17; CAMHS 9, 11; funding for 6, 10; numbers needing 6; referring on 6, 9, 10, 14, 17; under-funding 6, 10; waiting times 2, 116

staff supervision 37–9

stigma 7–8; impact of 7–8; lack of awareness of 12; and language of mental health 8; from peers 8; from teachers 8; normalising and 34

stress: impacts on the developing brain 61–2; levels of teacher 106–7; mitigators of 53, 66, 79, 83, 84, 109; negative impacts for pupils 84; negative impacts for teachers 36; positive impacts of 61; *see also* cortisol; buffer

teacher emotional labour 52, 86

teacher mental health *see* staff supervision; stress

teacher-pupil relationships *see* safeguarding; teacher qualities; teacher standards

teacher qualities: good enough teachers 107; good teachers 104–5; *see also* professional expectations of teachers

teachers' attachment styles *see* attachment

teenagers *see* adolescence

theory of mind *see* cognition

therapeutic schools: danger of 87; relationships in 84–6, 92; skills for 86–8

transgenerational trauma 16

trauma 28, 29–30, 36, 54, 86; trauma-informed 9

tribe 88; classroom 89, 90, 91; and compassion 47

understanding the behaviours of pupils 28–30; *see also* Crucial Cs

vulnerability 11, 14, 38, 86, 87, 109

Wales: approach to school support for mental health in 8, 9, 11, 12, 13, 14, 116; CAMHS in 6; curriculum in 14, 15, 88; equality legislation in 102; professional conduct in 105

window of tolerance *62*, *107*

Winnicott, D. *81*, *83*, *90*, *91*

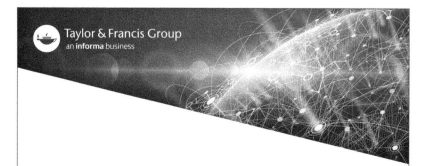

Printed in the USA
CPSIA information can be obtained
at www.ICGtesting.com
LVHW080737200324
774517LV00075B/811